‖‖‖‖‖‖‖‖‖‖‖‖‖‖‖‖‖‖‖‖‖
W9-BYD-715

THE
FIELD&
STREAM
Shooting Sports
Handbook

WITHDRAWN

The *Field & Stream* Fishing and Hunting Library

HUNTING

The Field & Stream *Bowhunting Handbook* by Bob Robb

The Field & Stream *Deer Hunting Handbook* by Jerome B. Robinson

The Field & Stream *Firearms Safety Handbook* by Doug Painter

The Field & Stream *Shooting Sports Handbook* by Thomas McIntyre

The Field & Stream *Turkey Hunting Handbook* by Philip Bourjaily

The Field & Stream *Upland Bird Hunting Handbook* by Bill Tarrant

FISHING

The Field & Stream *Baits and Rigs Handbook* by C. Boyd Pfeiffer

The Field & Stream *Bass Fishing Handbook* by Mark Sosin and Bill Dance

The Field & Stream *Fish Finding Handbook* by Leonard M. Wright, Jr.

The Field & Stream *Fishing Knots Handbook* by Peter Owen

The Field & Stream *Fly Fishing Handbook* by Leonard M. Wright, Jr.

The Field & Stream *Tackle Care and Repair Handbook* by C. Boyd Pfeiffer

THE
FIELD&STREAM
Shooting Sports Handbook

Thomas McIntyre

THE LYONS PRESS

EAU CLAIRE DISTRICT LIBRARY

T 118100

Copyright © 1999 by Thomas McIntyre

All rights reserved. No part of this book may be reproduced in any manner whatsoever without the express written consent of the publisher, except in the case of brief excerpts in critical reviews and articles. All inquiries should be addressed to: The Lyons Press, 123 West 18 Street, New York, NY 10011.

Printed in the United States of America

10 9 8 7 6 5 4 3 2 1

Library of Congress Cataloging-in-Publication Data

McIntyre, Thomas.
    The Field & stream shooting sports handbook / Thomas McIntyre
        p.   cm. — (Field & stream fishing and hunting library)
    ISBN 1-55821-915-3 (pb)
        1. Trapshooting Handbooks, manuals, etc.   2. Skeet shooting
Handbooks, manuals, etc.   I. Field & stream.   II. Title.
III. Title: Field and stream shooting sports handbook.   IV Title:
Shooting sports handbook.   V. Series.
GV1181.M34   1999
799.3'132—dc21   99-12871
                                                                            CIP

Contents

Acknowledgments

I wish to thank Nick Lyons, the Lyons Press, Slaton White, Mike Toth, David Petzal and all the staff of *Field & Stream*, and my editor, through thick and thin, Jay Cassell, for having brought this project to me. Beyond them, the individuals whose assistance contributed to the production of this book are simply too numerous to list. But to each of them, from all the shooting organizations, arms and ammunition manufacturers, and the makers of shooting accessories of every kind, my sincere thanks.

Preface

There are old sports and new. It would seem only logical that the fastest-growing sports in the United States would also be among the newest. After all, because they are just beginning, they have the most room to grow. So when the National Sporting Goods Association (NSGA) recently conducted a survey to find out what the fastest-growing sports are, it came as no great surprise that numbers one and two had some of the briefer histories in this country. Even so, these two sports, snowboarding and soccer, could be widely regarded as being most reflective of the supposed spirit of the times, because they seemed primarily designed to emphasize bustle and speed and had as their objective to get their participants nowhere fast.

So what might the third fastest-growing sport be? To judge by the first two, it could be assumed that it is something equally as "New Age" and "correct"; something perhaps even "holistic" and not merely modern but downright "*post*modern"; something also designed to move us along in a blur. In-line skating? Mountain biking? Whitewater kayaking? Actually, none of the above.

The third fastest-growing sport in this country is, instead, not just one of the oldest known in this nation but among the oldest known to man, one that can be traced to our very genesis as humans, to a skill we depended on for our very survival. Because at some point far back in our murky past we discovered the concept of "force at a distance": The ability to hurl or sling an object—whether a rock, a bone, a stick, a spear, or an arrow—at a target, generally something we were interested in eating. In this way we were able to extend the rather limited range of our arms and compensate for the slowness of our running stride.

The practice of this skill, though unquestionably physical and not without the need for swift reflexes and quick timing, also contains a substantial component of intense focus and steady nerves, perhaps more than any of the contemporary "motion" sports. In its modern

Target shooting is the third fastest-growing sport. *Remington Arms*

form, though, this skill is as capable of being practiced competitively by the old as by the young and by the less perfectly fit as by physical specimens. And it is this fundamental, prehistoric skill that is the essence of target shooting.

Today, according to a 1996 NSGA survey, almost 22 million Americans shoot at targets, devoting over 340 million days every year to, and spending literally billions of dollars on, the pastime. In addition, according to a 1996 survey by the National Shooting Sports Foundation (NSSF), one in five of the Americans who have never shot at targets would like to if ever offered the chance.

The growth of target shooting, or what can more broadly be thought of as the *shooting sports,* should really come as no surprise, though, if we think of it as part of a broader trend of setting aside some of the more hyperactive aspects of the times we live in and turning back to parts of our past that may have a more steadying effect on us. The shooting sports have the advantage of having originated with our most ancient ancestors. There is something about them we have sought and returned to over the millennia, something that sustains and reinforces us. Maybe part of it—no small part of it— is that at least one of the things the shooting sports represent and validate for us is a tradition we all too often forget to honor, the timeless tradition of child's play.

Among hunter-gatherers the playthings of the young always included toy spears and bows; and with these they first engaged in the game of shooting at targets, a game that taught them how to become proficient in obtaining food later in life. It was as an extension, or a prolongation beyond childhood, of this notion of play that caused people to come up with the idea as adults of shooting not just to collect meat but as a way of competing with one another. It was in this spirit that the ancient Greeks began the sport of "popinjay" shooting—which involved trying to hit a stuffed parrot, affixed to the top of a pole, with an arrow. And in Homer's *Odyssey,* there is a shooting competition in which Odysseus strings his powerful "backstrung bow" and shoots an arrow through 12 iron axes in a test of skill to prove he is a better man than all the suitors who have tried to claim his wife, Penelope, during his long absence at the Trojan War.

Armies as far back as the Romans used target practice as part of the regular training regimen of their troops. In 12th-century Japan, the Shogun, wanting stricter military training, ordered his soldiers to be drilled in shooting their bows while mounted on horses. The colorful and highly ritualized "game" that evolved from this drill was known as *yabusame* and is still practiced today.

In the Middle Ages, shooting contests with longbows and crossbows were a regular feature of village life, and this did not fade with the advent of firearms. One major development in firearms, in fact, the rifling of barrels, had its first applications in target shooting rather than in hunting or combat. Until the addition of rifling, though, along with better bullets, powders, and lock mechanisms, the firearm was considered a poor second to the bow in terms of power and accuracy. As late as the 1790s, matches between muskets and bows showed the bow to be the technologically superior weapon (indeed, the stock of the shoulder firearm grew out of the stock of the crossbow).

By the 19th century, though, with the invention of the percussion cap, rifling—and as odd as it may sound—the acceptance of the importance of *sights,* firearms completely displaced bows and arrows for almost every use, sporting and military. The Swiss developed an extremely heavy, large-bore, but very accurate rifle, known as the Schuetzen, especially for off-hand shooting at round wooden targets. In the United States, Americans were using their smaller-caliber "Kentucky" rifles in turkey shoots (or "rifle frolics"), where a gobbler would be tied up behind a log with its head the only exposed target.

The shotgun sports undoubtedly arose from there not being year-round bird hunting, combined with the constant, and irrepressible, urge gentlemen have to make a wager. Among the earliest competitive shotgun targets was the renaissance of the Greeks' popinjay, a live bird, tethered to a line that allowed it to fly short distances, frequently substituted for the stuffed one. The first mention of trap shooting, it is generally agreed, was in 1793 in England's *Sporting Magazine,* which is said to have described the activity as being "well established recreation."

The handgun sports, on the other hand, arose from forms of practice that were far from recreational. In the early part of the 1800s, very few people shot at targets with handguns for pleasure but rather to prepare for the possibility of having to defend themselves, either from brigands or in a duel, should they be challenged to one by an injured party.

Times have changed, of course; and many if not most handgunners (who, a survey says, number over 13 million, along with almost 12 million rifle shooters, 8 million shotgun shooters, and 3 million air gunners; and, let's not forget the 3 million muzzle loaders—many shooting with more than one of the various firearms, some with all, so overlap accounts for the 22-million net figure for participants in the shooting sports) shoot today for no better reason than the simple fun of it, without concern of assault or being drawn into single combat. And so we can see that the shooting sports are a way for us to return to the uncomplicated pleasures of those long-ago children. "Shooting sports," at their best, are nothing more than other words for that much misunderstood, but extremely necessary, human concept of play. So, let's play.

THE
FIELD&
STREAM
Shooting Sports
Handbook

PART

I

Shotgun Sports

Introduction

THERE IS A SHOTGUN GAME for almost any way that can be devised for making a target fly. Games with names like "Crazy Quail," "Rabbit Run," "Flurry," "Tower Shooting," "Starshot" (which looks like SWAT assaulting a Ferris wheel), and dozens more are played, with new ones being concocted on a regular basis. All the games, though, are essentially variations on the themes of what are called, rather sternly, the shotgun *disciplines,* of which there are three: trap, skeet, and sporting clays.

Trap, as we've seen, is by far the oldest of the disciplines, dating back in its earliest forms over 200 years. As well as being an Olympic event, in both singles and doubles (i.e., "singles" being only one target thrown at a time; "doubles" being two), trap is certainly the most

Olympic trapshooting. *USA Shooting*

Olympic skeet. *USA Shooting*

widely practiced of the shotgun disciplines—hardly a city or county in this country does not have some kind of trap field somewhere.

Skeet, also an Olympic shooting event, is nearly as widespread, even though it is more than a century younger. Before skeet even had a name, it was introduced as a "form of practice that is of real aid to the field shooter" because it claimed to simulate more accurately than trap the various lines of flight that a game bird might take, the clay birds in trap flying only away from the shooter. In skeet, the targets go away, come at, and cross in front of the shooter at varying angles, with singles and doubles being combined in the same round of shooting. Skeet is also, in keeping with its stated intention of honing hunting skills, the one discipline that has competition classes for the so-called sub-bore shotguns, specifically the 20 and 28 gauges and the .410. The only question is, Where did the name "skeet" come from?

Although it has been practiced for less than 20 years in this country, sporting clays has experienced a rate of growth more explosive than any of the other shotgun disciplines before it. Begun decades ago in England as a way for shooters (i.e., *hunters*) to replicate, even more than with skeet, the conditions of game shooting (i.e., *hunting*) during the off-season, sporting clays utilizes courses laid out over several acres of natural terrain and usually containing 10 to 14 stations

Sporting clays has experienced tremendous growth in recent years. *National Skeet Shooting Association*

that throw targets—varying in size from standard to minis (which in the air resemble black olives breaking Mach I)—in singles, pairs, and bouncing along the ground like some cwazy rabbit.

Before we look at the shotgun disciplines individually, we need to examine some of the fundamentals of shotgun shooting. As Americans, our shooting tradition comes out of the frontiersmen's use of their rifles to bring down large game, so it is not a great overstatement to say that the proper use of a shotgun is just a little foreign to us. And it is no overstatement to say that the only thing shooting a rifle and shooting a shotgun have in common is that they both involve firearms.

Rifle shooting is all about getting a "solid aim" and "lining up the sights." Movement is the bane of rifle shooting, but it is at the heart of shotgunning. Like the Sundance Kid, the shotgun shooter who does not move, and move properly, isn't going to hit a thing.

As we all learned in Shooting 101, unlike the single projectile of the rifle, the shotgun fires a large number of projectiles or pellets (shot), often several hundred depending on the gauge of the gun and the size of the pellets (a 12-gauge 1⅛-ounce load of No. 8 shot, for instance, would contain approximately 460 pellets). This shot forms a spreading "pattern" as it leaves the barrel, giving the shooter a greater chance of hitting a target in flight than he would have with a rifle bullet: Think of trying to kill a fly with a swatter rather than with a knitting needle. In order to cover a target with a shot pattern, a shooter cannot shoot at where the target is (because it is moving), but must send his shot ahead of the target to intercept it in flight. This involves swinging the shotgun barrel past the target so that it is pointing at a place in the air the proper distance ahead before firing. *(Shooting Tip: Following through, or continuing the swing after firing, is necessary to avoid unconsciously stopping the swing short.)* This, of course, is called lead, with shooters adopting one of three basic styles of leading—sustained (pointing ahead of the target and staying ahead through the swing), pulling away (pointing first at the target, then swinging past it), and swinging through (starting with the muzzle behind the target and *swinging through* it to get the lead). Each style has its advocates, and all shooters can do is try to find which works best for them.

As you may have noted, I have not used the term "aim" anywhere in conjunction with shooting a shotgun because a shotgun is never aimed (at least never should be) in the way a rifle is. A shotgun is all about *pointing* in just the way you point your finger at something, rather than aiming it. For this reason, a shotgun has no sights to align, at least none on the gun. The "sights" on a shotgun are the shooter's eye, lined up with the barrel. In order to point a shotgun properly, therefore, it is necessary that a shooter's "dominant eye" be the one that is lined up with the barrel; otherwise the barrel will always be off the target. For almost all of us one eye is, for lack of a better word, *stronger* than the other, and this is the eye that directs our vision. Usually, if we are right handed, it is our right eye, and if we are left handed, our left eye. But sometimes it is just the opposite, and many shooters never bother to learn which is their dominant eye.

The simplest test for determining your dominant eye is to pick out some small object (a doorknob or coffee cup will do) 10 or 15 feet away and look at it with both eyes open. Quickly extend your arm and point at the object with your index finger. *Freeze!* Now close one eye, then open it; then close the other eye. With one eye you should see your finger move off the object, while with the other it remains on it. Whichever eye, right or left, stays on the target is your dominant eye. Another method is to make an aperture with your two hands, then quickly raise and look through it. Now close one eye and then the other, and see which one is looking through the aperture.

If your dominant eye happens to be your right eye and you are right handed, you have no worries! The same is true for left eye/left handed. If you find, however, that you are "cross dominant," then you have several options (relax, one of them won't involve having to shoot in a frilly summer frock, patent-leather pumps, and a string of cultured pearls—unless you really want to). If you are just learning to shoot a shotgun, then learn to shoot from the side of your dominant eye; this, you will find in time, will be the most natural way of pointing. If you've been shooting for some time before learning of your cross dominance and have the patience and determination, you can still retrain yourself to shoot from the other side. If you don't want to go through that, then you can make your nondominant eye assume dominant duties.

The best way to do this involves blocking the center vision of your dominant eye while retaining the peripheral vision so vital to picking up targets in flight. Because you will always be wearing safety glasses when shooting your shotgun (see Chapter 5), an excellent method is to obscure a spot on the glasses that covers the pupil of your dominant eye. You want this spot to be no larger than necessary, so, **first making sure the shotgun is unloaded,** mount the gun to your shoulder and look down the barrel. While you are doing this, have another person place a small disk of frosted adhesive tape, no

Finding your dominant eye. *Photo by Elaine McIntyre.*

bigger than a dime, on the lens of your safety glasses directly over the pupil of your dominant eye. This will cause your nondominant eye, the one aligned with the shotgun barrel, to assume pointing duties. You can also daub a film of lip balm or something similar on the lens of the glasses over your pupil, or sometimes just slightly squinting your dominant eye will switch control to your nondominant one. At all costs, though, avoid shooting a shotgun with one eye completely closed.

Curiously, when your eye is properly aligned with the barrel of the shotgun, it should not be the barrel that it sees but the target. There is, in fact, no way of hitting a target in flight with a shotgun if you are looking at the barrel, anymore than a pitcher could hit the strike zone if he were looking at the baseball as he threw it. As in throwing a ball or pointing a finger, the eye goes to the target and the ball or finger, or shotgun barrel, goes to where the eye is looking.

Proper mounting of a shotgun is needed to make this possible. Finding a shotgun with the right dimensions, in length of pull (the distance from the trigger to the center of the butt: For a shooter of average build, usually around $14\frac{1}{2}$ inches), drop at the comb, and

Patching over your dominant eye. *Photo by Elaine McIntyre.*

drop at the heel (these are, basically, the amount of "bend" in the stock down from the line of the rib on the barrel or barrels: Varying according to the physique of the shooter, drop can be roughly anywhere from 1½ to 2½ inches), is very important, but is not a substitute for a shooter's knowing how to bring that gun to the shoulder.

The first element of a proper mount is a proper stance. On a trap or skeet field you can often witness shooters contorting themselves into outlandish postures—shoulders hunched up, chins thrust forward, backsides pouted out like Donald Duck's, assuming a crouch like that of the mighty jaguar about to pounce upon its unsuspecting prey, the gentle jungle tapir—and acting as if they actually know what they are doing. The fundamental stance for a shotgunner is very much like that of a boxer: The feet should be about shoulder width apart with the forward knee slightly bent, the hands raised ("put up your dukes!"), the elbows a comfortable distance away from the the sides (not sticking straight out, Funky Chicken style), the shoulders relaxed, the forward hand well forward, and the upper body leaning just far enough forward to have, as the saying goes, "nose over toes."

In most shotgun sports, shooters have the option of starting with their guns in a "low" position (the butt resting between elbow and

Low-gun position.

hip) or mounted to their shoulder before calling for a target to be thrown. For the new shooter, having to think about calling for a target, bringing the gun up, disengaging the safety, locating the target, getting on it, leading, and firing can be very complicated. A mounted gun can often help simplify matters and enable someone just starting out to break more birds and acquire greater confidence. *(Shooting Tip: In trap almost all shooters will want to begin with a mounted gun.)* As shooters gain more experience, they sometimes find that they can be even faster by moving slower, and so they will start from the low-gun position. The repetition of mounting the gun every time they yell "Pull!" makes them mount the gun correctly. Practiced shooters, for whom mounting the gun has become part of their muscle memory, may also find that starting from the low-gun position can help them pick up (that is, see) the target more quickly after it leaves the trap house, and so acquire it more smoothly.

In either way of holding a shotgun, the muzzle should cover the spot in the air where the shooter wants it to be when beginning the swing on the target. In bringing the shotgun up, the shooter first pushes the gun forward, raises the rear of the stock by lifting it with the trigger hand, and then pulls it firmly into the shoulder without tensing up. The shotgun's comb (the top of the rear stock) should

The comb of the stock must be solidly against the cheek.

come up solidly against the shooter's cheek without the shooter having to tilt the head over onto it, making sure the eyes remain level. Through all this, the forward hand remains essentially motionless, while the muzzle has not moved from where it was pointed at the sky. The shotgun should be at roughly a 45-degree angle to the line of the shoulders, compared to the perhaps 15- to 20-degree angle at which a rifleman holds his weapon across his chest, with the raised elbow of the trigger-hand arm creating a hollow in the shoulder for the shotgun butt to nestle in. *(Shooting Tip: Frequent, even persistent,* empty-gun *practice of the mounting routine at home is one of the best learning methods available, as is "dry-fire" practice for all the other shooting sports.)*

The shotgun should be swung by the pushing or pulling of the forward hand on the gun's fore-end. The speed of the swing can be controlled by how far out on the fore-end the forward hand is. Extended all the way, the barrel swings slower, but often more smoothly, whereas pulled closer in, the swing accelerates, often helping to overtake fast flyers. *(Shooting Tip: Mount the gun pointing directly at, or even just slightly past, the spot where you expect it to be when you pull the trigger. Then, without changing your foot placement, turn your body back toward the position where you expect first to pick up the target when it is thrown; this lets your body uncoil like a spring and is faster, and much less awkward, than trying to twist your body around in pursuit of a clay bird in flight.)* As important as following through on your lead is keeping your cheek planted on the comb, even after the shot. Other than that, never load your gun before taking your firing position, and never take off the safety before you are ready to fire.

Now it's time to step up to the line, but first let's look at what we will be stepping up to the line with and learn a little about its history.

Guns and Chokes

THE USE OF FIREARMS to shoot pellets, or shot, is a very old application of the gun. Early shot was laborious to make, and the result was crude, often being nothing more than chopped-up pieces of lead sheet. The shooting it provided was equally crude, with pot hunters using their shotguns to splatter flocks of wildfowl on the ground or water and bagging not just two birds with one stone, but often tens of birds with one shot. "Sport" was hardly a consideration until the shotgun became more reliable and more refined. When gentlemen had proved to themselves that shooting game on the wing, or "shooting flying," as it was known, was possible, then it became fashionable.

A flintlock mechanism.

EAU CLAIRE DISTRICT LIBRARY

Shooting flying did not become a reality until the perfecting of the first really trustworthy firing mechanism, the flintlock. The Norman artist and gunsmith Marin le Bourgeoys is generally credited with having de-bugged the flintlock by incorporating the frizzen and pan cover in a single piece of steel—thus helping to keep the priming powder dry—and internalizing the lock's works. So when a fowler swung on a bird in the air and touched off his shot, the gun might actually fire, and with a fast enough lock time (the interval between the dropping of the flint on the frizzen and the ignition of the powder charge behind the load of shot) the shooter might be confident that the shot would reach where he was pointing in time to meet up with the bird.

Yet another advancement in the practice of wingshooting came about in 1769. It was then that the Englishman William Watts devised a method of manufacturing shot of uniform size. His method involved dropping lead in molten form from a high tower through sieves with varying-size openings (depending on the size of shot desired) into vats of water. The sieves were made to vibrate, causing the lead to form into globules that were further rounded into perfect little spheres by their passage through the air. (Watts, it is said, came to his discovery by way of a dream.)

Flintlocks and uniform shot worked well enough until shooters began to notice that the flash of the priming powder in the pan would often alert birds that a load of that shot was heading their way and cause them to veer radically. One wildfowler who was tired of seeing ducks flare every time he pulled the trigger was the Reverend Dr. Alexander John Forsyth, minister of Belhelvie parish, Aberdeenshire, Scotland. As a solution to the problem, in 1807 he patented the percussion "scent-bottle" lock, which used fulminate—an explosive substance derived from dissolving metals in acids—instead of flint and priming powder to ignite the blackpowder charge in a gun. In Forsyth's system, the priming charge of fulminate (usually fulminate of mercury and saltpeter) was held in a closed chamber and was struck and detonated with a "plug or sliding-piece so as to exclude the open air, and to prevent any sensible escape of the blast." Thus internalized, the ignition of the powder charge was not only invisible to passing birds but far more efficient than any previous system.

The next major development in shotgunning was the choke. Since the projectiles in a shotgun leave the muzzle in what is essentially a spray, like water leaving a hose, it stood to reason that spray could be regulated hydromechanically as well. Think of the nozzle on a garden hose and you have the basic principal of the choke: The more the constriction (up to a point), the "tighter" the spray, or "pattern," of shot and the longer its useful range. While Fred Kimble, an old-time Illinois market gunner, is often said to have been the inventor of the choke (he *was* a great popularizer of it), it was actually the Amherst, Massachusetts, gunsmith Sylvester H. Roper who on April 10, 1866, first patented an effective choke.

Roper's design consisted of an attachment that screwed onto the muzzle of a single-barreled shotgun and reduced the diameter of the bore. It worked, although not as well as the permanent choking that could be done in the shotgun barrels of the time. And yet, with modern advancements in technology and design, the interchangeable choke that screws on, or rather "screws in," the muzzle has today become the standard method of choking shotguns.

To make possible the rapid-fire shotgun sports we know today, a method of loading had to be devised that was faster than pouring powder and shot down the muzzle of a shotgun. The result, of course, was the breech-loading shotgun along with the shotgun cartridge that had primer, powder, wad, and shot in one self-contained package. The first breech-loading percussion gun was patented in 1831 by the Parisian gunsmith Augustus Demondion, whereas the patent for a priming system integral with the base of a cartridge dates back to another Paris gunsmith, Houiller, in 1847. Smokeless powder began being used in shotgun shells even before the close of the Civil War. By 1874, the first ejector double-guns were available, followed the next year by the first hammerless shotguns, made by Anson and Deeley in England. Brass cartridges began to be replaced by paper; the slide-action, or "pump," shotgun and the autoloader appeared on the scene; and somebody found an electrical outlet in which to plug the throwing machine.

Today we can choose from five types of shotguns for use in the shooting sports. These fall it two categories: the break-actions and the repeaters. The break-actions include the single-barreled, the double-barreled side-by-side (or, simply, double), and the double-barreled over-and-under (over-and-under or even stack barrel). And there are two types of repeaters: slide-action (also called a pump, as stated above), and the autoloader (auto, or, more correctly, semiauto). Let's briefly review the pros and cons of these guns.

Double barrel—the classic shotgun design.

The double is the classic shotgun design going back to the flint-lock shotguns of Joseph Manton, the 18th-century patron saint of English best-gun makers, his being the first great recognizable talent and brand name to be sought after. As a game gun the double is a superb choice (I'd rather take my own quick-handling Browning double out after wild quail than any other gun I own), but it is probably not the gun for serious competition (if it were, you'd see them being used, and you simply do not). The over-and-under is a much better choice, perhaps even the best, for the shooting sports for two fundamental reasons. First, the single-sighting plane along the barrel of the over-and-under allows shooters to see more of the target area and to pick up the target faster, their vision unobscured by the width of two barrels; and second, the gun's straight-line recoil lets shooters keep their eyes on the target without having the barrel jump up in the face, an important factor when shooting doubles—targets, not guns. An added consideration, more so for single-barreled guns than for double, is that the increased weight of the stacked barrels helps produce smoother, more controlled swings.

If the over-and-under is not the best choice for a shooting-sports

Over-and-under shotgun—the preferred choice for most shooting sports. *USA Shooting*

gun, it is only because it runs neck and neck with the autoloader. Modern autoloaders, if well maintained, are as reliable as break-action guns (or rather, *almost*, nothing being more reliable than a good-quality break-action). Their action directs recoil back in a straight line, reducing muzzle jump, whereas the automatic process of ejecting the empty hull and loading a new cartridge greatly softens the gun's kick. The pump, however, lets the shooter absorb all the recoil and slows the second shot by making the shooter have to work the action before firing. It also presents the shooter with the risk of "short shucking" a shell—that is, failing to move the slide far enough back to eject the empty hull before pushing it forward to load the next cartridge. Nonetheless, many top competitors have shot very well with the pump; but with continuing improvements in the autoloader, trying to compete in anything but Singles or Handicap Targets in trapshooting with a "trombone" gun is a little like tying on hiking boots to run a 100-yard dash.

For the serious trapshooter uninterested in shooting doubles, there remains the single-barreled shotgun with its specialized stock and rib. Long-barreled and tightly choked, it is meant for breaking

Remington Model 1100 Synthetic shotgun. *Remington*

Remington Model 870 TC trap. *Remington*

birds at distance. But how long is long, how tight is tight, and what does "at distance" mean?

There may be an application for a barrel nearing a yard in length and for severe choking on a shotgun destined for shooting trap; but too many shooters believe that long barrels and tight chokes are the answer to all their needs in the shotgun-shooting sports. I think that anyone taking up the shotgun sports, or even those who have been in them for a time, should proceed with caution before running out to buy a shotgun with a 34-, 32-, or even 30-inch barrel and a fixed full choke, unless he is entirely sure, without fear of contradiction, that this is the right gun for his shooting situation.

Chokes, of course, come in differing amounts of constriction, which are labeled Cylinder, no constriction; Improved Cylinder, a tightening of .010 inches from the bore's standard diameter (.729 inches in the case of the 12 gauge); Modified, .020 inches; and Full, .035 inches. Besides these basic four amounts of constriction, there are such subtle distinctions as Skeet, .005 inches, running through Light Modified, Improved Modified, Light Full, all the way to Extra Full which cranks the barrel diameter down .040 inches. The function of any choke is to deliver the optimum dispersal—that is, the spray, pattern, or "spread" of shot at a desired range. For hunting purposes, this is usually defined as all the shot, evenly distributed, placed within a 30-inch circle at 40 yards, but this is not necessarily the case with the shotgun sports.

PATTERN/PELLET DENSITY & ENERGY GUIDE

Look up distance to your game for recommended pellet. Pellets appropriate for longer distances may also be used at shorter range. Use of pellets at distances surpassing their listing is not recommended.

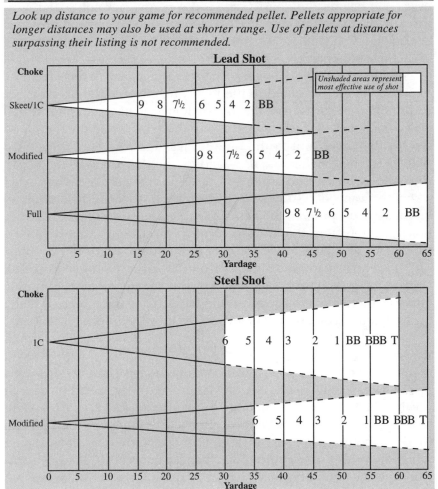

Courtesy of *Black's Wing & Clay.*

In the shotgun sports, targets have their own ideal yardages at which they can be most easily broken, depending on which sport is being played, so the choke needs to be matched to that yardage. As Chuck Webb, gunsmith, skeet shooter, and general manager of Briley, one of the country's oldest manufacturers of custom and after-market interchangeable chokes, puts it, picking a choke is "like choosing a golf club." And yet most people seem to want to use too much choke and too much barrel in most of their shooting, like wanting to hit every golf ball on the course with a driver. Another consideration is the way the target presents itself, so to explain yardage and presentation and how they relate to choke selection, let's turn to the situation found in trapshooting.

In the trapshooting game known as Singles, which will be explained in greater depth in the following chapter, a shooter stands at a position 16 yards from the low building called the traphouse and calls for a target to be thrown. The trap machine inside the traphouse throws the target, and in the time it takes the shooter to react—to pick up the bird, swing, and fire—and for the shot to reach the target, the target is, on average, around 32 yards from the shooter. Now, what a shooter wants is for the load of shot when it reaches the target to be filling that optimum 30-inch circle, both because there are fewer holes in the pattern that the target might slip through and because a trap target, as it flies away, presents itself either "edge-on" or "dome-on." Both presentations happen to be the hardest profiles to break because of their narrowness and because the edge and the outside curve of the dome are the most durable parts of the target, so that a lot of shot is needed to break birds when they fly in these positions.

Is a Full choke, then, the best choice for delivering the largest, densest pattern of, say, No. 8 shot at that 32-yard range? More likely it would be the choice at 45 yards. Then how about Modified? Maybe this is the one to use at 40 yards. According to the choke chart put out by Gil Ash, a noted shotgunning authority, at 32 yards, a Light Modified would probably be the right choice for trap. In trapshooting there is another game, as we shall also see, known as Handicap, in which shooters fire from positions that can go as far back as 27 yards from the traphouse; but even all the way back there, you're still not likely to need more than a Modified choke.

The point is not to get caught up in the mythology that more barrel and more choke are always better; they may even be worse. If you buy that 34-inch trap gun with the Extra Full choke, it may not be easy to have that choke opened up later on. An essential part of any choke is the taper, or "cone" or "lede," of the barrel that precedes the parallel-sided constricted section at the muzzle. This taper needs to be ¾ inch in length in order to let the shot make a smooth transition from the barrel to the choke. Opening a choke from its original diameter may shorten this taper and cause the shot load to become disrupted and not leave the shotgun in the uniform cluster necessary for

Interchangeable chokes.

proper patterning. The sensible choice, especially when new to the shooting sports, is to buy a gun with barrels, or a barrel, no longer than 28 inches; interchangeable chokes; and more or less standard (i.e., average) dimensions and features. Then take the gun out, set up a patterning board, and test various chokes and loads at different yardages until you find which combinations work best in your gun for the different types of shooting you plan to do. This may be time consuming, but for anyone serious about the shooting sports it is a much faster, cheaper, and far less frustrating way of finding how your gun shoots than through round after round of abysmal scores, with more zeros attached to your name than to the national debt.

CHAPTER 3

Trapshooting

A T THIS POINT, there is not much more that can be learned about shotguns without actually shooting one, and about the best way to do so is in the most time-honored of the shotgun sports, trapshooting.

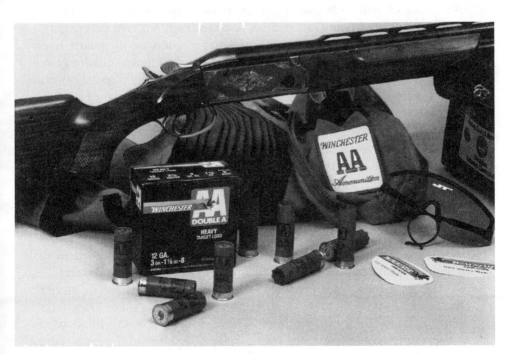

Basic trapshooting equipment. *Winchester*

Trapshooting has been old hat, literally, almost from its inception. In the early 1800s, many shoots, well attended by the à la mode betting men of the period, were held at the Uxbridge Road public house, "Old Hats," near London. The pub earned its sobriquet because the live wild pigeons used in the matches were placed in holes in the ground that were then covered by old hats. When the shooter called for a bird, a puller yanked on a string attached to the hat, allowing the bird to fly up. In other locales the holes were covered with wooden planks that were pulled up. Eventually a box, whose sides and top would fly out and lie flat when a string was pulled, was used to contain, or "trap," the bird. The first place where such traps were used, and the first genuine pigeon-shooting club, was at Hornsey Wood House in England, the club said to have been founded in 1810.

Despite almost continuous complaints about the inhumanity of using live animals for target practice, live-pigeon shooting remained an enormously popular sport throughout the 19th century and into the 20th (the English Parliament outlawed it in 1921). It continues today, both legally and illegally, in many countries, including the United States, with substantial purses being available for top guns and handsome sums being wagered on the contests. No two pigeons fly alike, and it is this unpredictability that for good or ill makes live-pigeon shooting such a fascinating, and certainly a highly challenging, shooting sport. By the middle of the 1800s, though, trapshooters were looking for alternatives to real pigeons, both because of mounting public distaste for their pastime and because of the disappearance of their feathered targets.

This scarcity was more pronounced in the United States than in England because of the dwindling number of passenger pigeons, which were the American trapshooters' primary target. One of the first substitutes for pigeons, just after the Civil War, came out of Boston where a Charles Portlock is said to have introduced glass balls as targets. Portlock, who supposedly drew his idea from the glass floats used on Japanese fishing nets, devised a spring-loaded mechanism to launch the balls, though not, some say, in a very satisfactory manner.

The glass balls were first clear, then stained green, blue, or amber (the better to be seen); then feathers were pasted on them. They later came to be stuffed with feathers, with some even being filled with gunpowder, all to create more spectacular effects when the balls were broken. The balls were relatively easy to hit, at least compared to live pigeons: Captain Adam H. Bogardus, one of the 19th century's great shotgunners and the first man documented to have killed 100 pigeons straight, in the late 1870s broke 5,681 balls without a miss during an exhibition; Annie Oakley in that same event distinguished herself by breaking 4,772 out of 5,000. However, the balls often didn't break, the shot glancing off them, so they were given a raised, checkered pattern on the outside to catch the shot better and break more easily.

The next, and permanent, alternative to the glass balls for trap shooting (and, in fact, for the rest of the shotgun sports) was the clay pigeon or clay bird, or as it is now known, the clay target, and breaking was sometimes also a problem for the early designs (although another noted shotgunner of the 1800s, the trick-shot "Doc" Carver, broke 60,616 during an exhibition in 1885 that lasted from Monday until Thursday evening). Sometime around 1870, disks made of (no peeking!) *clay* began to be thrown for shotgunners, but these often proved too soft, breaking up in flight, or too hard, merely ringing, it's been said, "like a bell" when struck. Apparently, a number of individuals, among them a George Ligowsky of Cincinnati, Fred Kimble, the

Clay targets come in a variety of sizes.

Laporte 285 Twinlap trap machine. *Laporte*

man who didn't invent the choke, and an Englishman named
McCaskey, began working independently on improving the clay target, as well as coming up with better mechanical throwers to get the
"birds" airborne. The final result, and the one trapshooters break
today, was a domed saucer made from petroleum pitch and gypsum.
The clay target's dome shape created aerodynamic lift, in the same
manner as the upper curved surface of an airplane's wing, allowing it
to sail smoothly for a considerable distance.

The official clay target shot in trap today can be no larger than
$4^{5}/_{16}$ inches in diameter and $1^{1}/_{8}$ inches in height. The machine for
throwing clay targets is still known as the trap, but today at most trap
ranges it is operated electrically rather than manually. (Some traps
have become so technologically sophisticated that they are able to be
activated by an individual shooter's voice and no other sound.) A trap
must throw a target between 48 and 52 yards (44 and 52 for doubles), measured "on level ground in still air," according to the book of
rules for trap. This is roughly at 65 miles an hour, or about the flight
speed of a pheasant.

The trap is set in the so-called traphouse where it is concealed from the shooters, the machine oscillating back and forth while stopping and starting at irregular intervals so a shooter can never be certain at what angle the target will leave the trap. Sixteen yards back from the trap, as described earlier, is the firing line, with five shooting positions, or stations, arranged in an arc, three yards between each position. Each position has individual yard markers running from 16 yards to 27 yards behind it. A shooter must stand behind the 16-yard marker in position when shooting regular Singles. Five shooters, or a "squad," shoot in sequence, with the shooter in position No. 1 firing once at his first target, followed by the shooter in position No. 2 firing at his, and so on, rotating through the lineup until each shooter has fired five shots, at which time the shooter moves to the next position in the order 1, 2, and so on, with the shooter in position 5 going to position 1. At the end of a round, each shooter will have fired five shots from each position for a total of 25 shots.

A target can be scored either "Dead" or "Lost." A target is Dead, and therefore is scored as a hit, if a shooter breaks any visible piece of it,

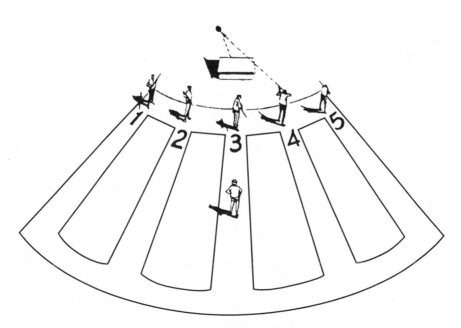

Layout of trap field. Courtesy of *Black's Wing & Clay*.

or disintegrates it, but is Lost if no piece of it is broken or if a shooter manages only to raise dust off it. A Dead target is scored with an "X," whereas a Lost one is designated by the notorious "O," the ol' goose egg. (Targets in skeet and sporting clays are scored in the same manner.) To score a hit, the shooter must also break the target within bounds, which in the case of trap means within an angle of a little more than 84 degrees, the vertex being the trap machine.

Organized trapshooting using live pigeons began in the United States probably in the 1820s, and it wasn't until the 1880s that clay birds began to replace animate ones. Over the next decade, the sport was formalized along the lines described above, and what we would recognize as the first trapshooting tournaments began to be held.

Two events marked the year 1900 as a pivotal one in trapshooting. One was the founding of the American Trapshooting Association, the name changing in 1923 to the Amateur Trapshooting Association (ATA). The ATA, with a current membership of over 50,000, is the governing body for trapshooting in this country.

The second event was the first Grand American World Trapshooting Championships, the ATA's main tournament, held in June 1900 in Interstate Park in Queens, New York. (Because there were only 20 competitors in that first tournament, it did not refer to itself as the "world" championships but chose the simpler, and somewhat more modest, title Grand American.) For the next 20 years, the Grand American was held in various cities, including Chicago and St Louis, until in 1924 it found a permanent home in Vandalia, Ohio, north of Dayton. Today, the Grand American is described as among the "oldest and richest sporting events" in America, "the largest participation sporting event in the world," and the world's "largest shooting event"—outside of global conflicts, one assumes. However it is described, the Grand American, over the course of 10 days, manages to draw more than 6,000 competitors, going after $175,000 in prize monies, and 100,000 spectators to Ohio in the swelter of August!

Whatever the impact of the Grand American and the ATA, trapshooters across the country today shoot at over 80 million targets each year—and those are just the ones that are registered by the 1,200 ATA-affiliated gun clubs. The total number might be something closer to a half billion, if one includes all the nonregistered targets that get shot at by the millions who visit trap ranges several times a year and who help to make trapshooting a $250-million sport in this country.

Most people, of course, are shooting 16-Yard Singles, as just described, although some are shooting Doubles, in which two clay targets are thrown simultaneously. The third trapshooting event is, as mentioned earlier, Handicap Targets, in which a shooter starts at the 19-yard mark and is then assigned longer yardages, depending on proficiency, going all the way back to the "fence" at 27 yards. The scoring percentage over at least 1,000 targets is the measure used to determine the shooter's handicap.

Another rare form of trap is known as International (sometimes European), Bunker, or Olympic, although it is not shot in the Olympics—only Singles and Doubles are—and is considered perhaps the most difficult of the shotgun sports. Found in only a handful of trapshooting ranges around the country, International uses 15 traps set in a trench, five stations, and a six-person squad of shooters with five shooting and one on deck, two shots allowed at each target, which must fly 77 yards (or roughly a lot faster than a regular trap target), with misses announced by the blast of an air horn. Well, believe me, if you're reading this book, you've probably never shot it, and I would have no idea where to begin to tell you how.

To shoot the saner brands of trap, though, there are a few things to keep in mind. The first is that in trap the bird is continually increasing the distance between you and it as soon as it leaves the traphouse. This means that it is to your advantage to get onto a target as quickly as possible. It is helpful, then, to anticipate where the target may first appear when it leaves the traphouse and have your gun pointing near that spot. You cannot, of course, guess the exact spot, but you do know that the bird is not going to appear out of the cinder blocks from the back of the traphouse or somewhere out there at the top of the treeline or in the clouds passing over the sun or 90 degrees off to your left. You want your gun pointing in what is essentially the middle of the target's possible flight path. If you are standing at the center, or No. 3, station, then where to point is very simple: about a foot high, directly over the middle of the traphouse. Going back to the No. 1 station, you want to point about a foot over the front-left corner (as seen from the shooting position) of the traphouse; No. 2, between the No. 1 and No. 3 holds; No. 4, between No. 3 and the front-right corner; and No. 5 above the front-right corner. This will not put you precisely on every target every time, but it will keep you close enough to the target that you will be able to pick it up in a

Remington Premier STS 12-Gauge Pigeon (cutaway). *Remington*

minimum amount of time and with a minimum amount of move-ment. *(Shooting Tip: You will want to adjust your stance at each station to give yourself the widest range of stable movement for covering the target's flight, so that if it goes left, for example, you won't be out of position by having your body turned too far to the right.)*

Now, as far as choosing which shotgun to use to learn to shoot trap, there are really only a few factors you need to take into consid-eration, most of which we've already looked at. One thing to remem-ber about trapshooting, though, is that it makes no allowances for smaller gauges, the rules stating only that a shotgun must be no larger than 12 gauge. A cartridge used for trapshooting may be loaded with no more than 3 drams equivalent of smokeless powder and 1⅛ ounces of lead shot no larger than No. 7½, as defined by the Sporting Arms and Ammunition Manufacturers' Institute (SAAMI), a load that is pretty well standard for the 12 gauge. So unless you are very small in stature or extremely recoil shy (and if loaded to full capacity, a 20 gauge, for instance, isn't going to "kick" a whole lot less than a 12 gauge, particularly if you start out with a light 12-gauge load), there's no reason not to use a 12 gauge. Besides, if you ever happen make it to the Grand American, you'll have to use a 12 gauge.

For the expert, a gun designed exclusively for trapshooting can be among the most specialized of shotguns, frequently having a bar-rel measuring 32 inches and even longer. It is often, if only, used for 16-Yard or Handicap, single shot and can be configured with a raised "Monte Carlo" stock and a high, ventilated rib that in profile looks like a suspension bridge (being of most use to shooters who like to adopt a very straight, "heads-up" posture). Choking varies but tends toward the tighter side, which may not always be to the average shooter's advantage, as has been discussed, but this is the expert we are talking about here, not the average Joe. Because a pure trap gun, really applicable to no other shotgun sport, can represent an investment of $2,000 to $3,000, and at the farthest end of the spectrum many times that, just be certain of how much of an expert you actually are before you run out to buy one.

CHAPTER

Skeet

W HILE THE ORIGINS OF TRAP are Old World and old hat, skeet can trace its ancestry to an Andover, Massachusetts, dog kennel and a group of bird hunters looking for a way to pass the time after the close of the 1915 season. In a pasture they drew a large circle and marked off 12 evenly spaced positions. They then placed a trap machine at high noon, throwing toward 6 o'clock, and shot at two targets each from stations No. 1 through No. 11, using up the last three shells from their boxes of 25 by standing in the center of the circle and shooting at the clay birds jetting overhead. They informally called this new sport, aptly enough, shooting "around the clock."

While the trap machine had to throw a target only one way, the shooters, as they moved from station to station, had 12 distinct angles from which to try to hit it. After a while someone noticed that by using a circle, the shooters were, half the time, shooting back toward buildings and houses, so they bisected the circle and added a second trap machine at 6 o'clock, throwing back toward 12 o'clock. On this semicircle, which now resembled a section of an orange, they placed eight stations. The layout for a skeet field evolved into the following official dimensions: The circle has a radius of 21 yards, with stations 1 through 7 set equidistant on the outside of that radius precisely 26 feet, 8⅜ inches apart; station 8 is set in the center of a base line, or "base chord," drawn between 1 and 7. Of the two traps set in "skeet-houses," one, the "high house," is set 3 feet beyond the marker for station 1 and 10 feet off the ground; the second, the "low house," is set 3 feet beyond marker 7 and 3½ feet above the ground.

The sport itself consisted of shooting at two single targets (the trap machine was set to throw 60 yards), one from each house, then a

33

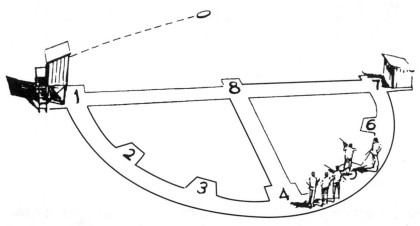

Skeet field layout. Courtesy of *Black's Wing & Clay.*

crossing double, with, again, one from each house, at stations 1 and 2 and 6 and 7. At stations 3 through 5, only a pair of singles were thrown. At 8, the shooter had a pair of singles, one from each house, that he had to break before they passed the stake marking the "target crossing point" at the center of the base chord. Some quick math shows that this accounts for only 24 shots, although a round of skeet consisted of 25. The extra shot was taken immediately after the first miss, at the same target as the one missed; if no targets were missed after 24, it was added to the infamous No. 8 low house—more on which later. (In International Skeet, which is the type shot at the Olympics, the optional target is eliminated by reshuffling the singles and doubles at each station; targets fly 72 yards, and guns must be kept in the low position until a target appears, and that target can appear at any time within three seconds of the shooter's calling "Pull!")

Articles in sporting magazines about this new sport (which had yet to be given an official name) began to appear in 1920, and by 1926 the basic rules had been formulated. Still, it needed to be called something catchy, so a contest to name the game was held. The winner, out of 10,000 entries, was a Mrs. Gertrude Hurlbutt of Dayton, Montana, who submitted the word "skeet," taken from the old Scandinavian word for "shoot," and walked away with the munificent prize of $100. Well publicized, skeet grew rapidly, and in 1946 the National Skeet Shooting Association (NSSA) was formed as the nonprofit governing body of the sport. Today NSSA membership is some 20,000 with over 2 million people a year shooting skeet at one of the association's 1,000 affiliated ranges. Every October the biggest event in skeet shooting, the World Skeet Championships, is held in San Antonio, Texas, attracting more than 1,400 participants.

The great allure of skeet, initially, was the premise that it provided more realistic off-season practice for bird hunters than did trap. Frankly, I believe this aspect of the sport is overrated, perhaps even extremely so. Skeet certainly does not make anyone a *worse* bird shooter, but what it does make one, above all, is a better *skeet* shooter. A look at the basic dimensions of a skeet field show that it is unlikely you are going to shoot at, let alone break, any target beyond 25 yards, and most targets at probably less than 15 yards. The targets fly unerringly on prescribed paths, so it is entirely possible to take out your pocket calculator and determine what the exact physical lead should be for any shot before the target ever appears in the air. And a good bit of the time those targets are coming more or less

Shooting skeet.

toward the shooter, "back lipped," as it is called—that is, with their undersides, the most vulnerable part, exposed. If ducks, or any birds, flew this way and came only when I called for them and had my shotgun up and ready to shoot, then, yes, skeet would be great practice for hunting birds, except that birds like that would have become extinct ages ago.

All this is to say that the value of skeet does not lie in its pedagogical qualities for making us better hunters. It is perfectly all right to enjoy skeet as nothing more than what it is (a sport of shooting at clay targets), rather than because it is supposedly something that is "good for us."

A skeet gun and skeet choke are probably more applicable to hunting, though, than a trap gun is, particularly the more specialized trap guns. Skeet guns have 26- to 28-inch barrels, as a rule, and are choked much more open. Many hunters, particularly of upland game, look for these features in their shotguns. The best chokes for skeet are, logically enough, Skeet or even Cylinder. As in trap, 12-gauge shells can be loaded with a maximum of $1\frac{1}{8}$ ounces of lead shot, ranging in size from No. 9 to $7\frac{1}{2}$. Unlike trap, skeet does make provisions for the smaller gauges, the 20, 28, and .410; these guns are allowed to fire $\frac{7}{8}$, $\frac{3}{4}$, and $\frac{1}{2}$ ounce of shot, respectively. Many shooters like to compete in all four gauge categories and so will often choose shotguns fitted with four interchangeable sets of barrels so they can maintain the consistent feel of shooting the same shotgun, no matter the size of the shell.

Lead, while important in trap, figures more in skeet. The assorted methods of leading have been described, and although it is possible to give specific distances for leading specific targets, such numbers are not very helpful since the perception of lead is a highly subjective matter, with no two shooters able to estimate a fixed distance exactly alike. A shooter learns leading through shooting. It also helps to have a qualified observer watch a shooter and see if the person is in front of or behind the proper lead. (As explained earlier, one way to regulate lead is by positioning the forward hand on the fore-end: The farther the hand is extended, the slower the lead, whereas drawing the hand in can sometimes help pick up the lead on faster birds).

Of all the shots in skeet, those at station No. 8, particularly at the low house, can appear utterly impossible to beginning shooters. There seems to be no way to pick up the bird as it leaves the skeet-house, find the lead, and break it before it passes the crossing stake, and there isn't. Breaking the targets at No. 8 is almost entirely mechanical and is accomplished by the shooter's pointing the muzzle just below and slightly to the outside of the opening in the skeethouse. Then, when the shooter calls for the target and it appears, the shooter simply swings the barrel of the shotgun along the line of the target's flight, and when the muzzle is pointing overhead, pulls the trigger. When a shooter finally catches the timing, the target will vanish almost every time into a cloud of fine black dust, creating what is one of the more satisfying experiences in all the shooting sports, even if it is mostly a trick.

CHAPTER 5

Gear

BEFORE MOVING ON to sporting clays, let's take a brief interlude to examine one of the stronger motivations for starting in on the shooting sports. One of the somewhat guilty pleasures of taking up any new sport is the joy of acquiring all sorts of nifty new equipment. Many of the items shooters buy, though, go beyond the realm of gear, past gadgets, and all the way out to gizmos. Take those brilliant, fiber-optic beads some shooters put on their shotguns. These may be marvelous for helping you see the end of your barrel, but as we have already noted, and will emphasize again, the point is not to see the end of your barrel but to see your target. Some items, however, are essential for all shooters, in whichever of the shooting sports they choose to participate.

The most essential piece of equipment is protective eyewear. The likelihood of getting hit by the shot from another's shotgun on a well-controlled shooting range is admittedly extremely slight, yet it can happen. More often, though, gases or bits of unburnt powder or even tiny shavings of metal can blow back into a shooter's face after firing a shotgun, not to mention the rare possibility of some catastrophic failure of the gun or ammunition, resulting in a blow up. Impact-resistant glasses for shooting, then, make as much sense as seat belts in a car.

Shooting glasses come in a number of tints, each applicable to different shooting conditions. There are clear glasses as well as smoke-tinted ones for bright days. Amber and vermillion work well on cloudy days or under other low-light conditions, whereas target-orange tints help shooters pick up orange targets in flight. Shooters who normally wear glasses can use them at the range, but they should make sure that they can withstand impact without shattering.

Protective eyewear. *Zeiss*

Though not always considered so, protecting one's hearing is just as important as protecting one's sight. For years shooters did not worry about the effect the repeated report of a firearm might have on their hearing, which is why there are so many functionally deaf shooters walking around shooting ranges these days, engaging in shouted conversations with one another. If anything, with the increased use of muzzle brakes (see later in this chapter) on firearms, the situation has become worse. Using earplugs at all times while on a shooting range is a good practice; wearing muff-type hearing protectors that cover the entire ear is even better; the ideal is to use both. Because the noise of the firearm is one of the factors that adds to the recoil a shooter perceives, "double plugging," by significantly muffling this sound, also helps to prevent flinching when the shooter fires at a target.

Earmuffs. *Remington*

PC 27 insert plugs for hearing protection. *Remington*

Beyond eyesight and hearing protection, other pieces of gear become a little less mandatory. Something in which to hold shells while walking from station to station is very useful, and this can either be some kind of holder worn on a belt or the pockets of a shooting vest. A vest has the added advantage of offering a shooter extra shoulder padding. If a shooter intends to use a low-gun position before mounting the shotgun, a "Continental" style vest with a full-length leather shooting pad will help prevent the recoil pad's snagging as the gun is raised.

Shooting gloves are not a bad idea, either. They can help a shooter keep a grip on the shotgun when the palms might be sweaty due to heat or the tension of competition. Gloves can be full length or fingerless, as long as they cover the second joint of the middle finger of

Shooting gloves.

the shooting hand; this finger can often get banged up by the trigger guard, and padding it will prevent painful bruising.

To prevent "bruising" your shotgun, a case is a very good idea. For transporting your gun between your house and the range, a padded, zippered soft case will work well. If you are going to travel long distances with your gun, and when traveling anywhere with it by commercial airplane, you will need a hard-sided, airline-approved carrying case that locks.

Sensible shoes are right up there on the equipment list. If you plan on walking over a good bit of rough ground, as when, say, you are making your way around a sporting-clays course, then light hiking boots might be in order. But on the level concrete of a trap or skeet field, any shoe that gives a solid, stable platform from which to shoot will do; even a good pair of running shoes will fit that job description.

One last item: For your shotgun, you might want a muzzle brake. This is a series of vents, or ports, that are machined into the muzzle of the shotgun and direct the exhaust gases out the sides of the muzzle, helping to lengthen the period of recoil and therefore lessen its sensation. In other words, instead of the recoil coming in one sharp jolt,

Hard-sided shotgun case. *Swanson Russell Assoc.*

a muzzle brake spreads it out over a longer period of time, making the recoil feel more like a shove than a punch. One drawback of a muzzle brake is an increase in muzzle blast, but more sophisticated designs for these gas ports are even helping to reduce that, or at least redirect them away from the shooter.

CHAPTER

Sporting Clays

ANYONE THINKING OF taking up sporting clays should be given fair warning: This sport may be habit forming.

Some years ago, Jim, a Texas dove-and-quail hunter, got talked into shooting a round. ("Jim's" name has been changed to protect the guilty.) Finding trap and skeet boring, he did not hold out much hope for sporting clays. After that first round, though—shooting from a series of stations at targets that flushed or crossed or soared or decoyed or *ran*—he walked up to the course manager and told him he'd be back.

Great, said the manager. The course was open several days a week, and . . .

"No," said Jim, "you don't understand. I'm going to town to get more shells. I'll be *right* back."

Poor Jim became so addicted to sporting clays that he has now become a Level III instructor (the highest level) in sporting clays, and shooters who are not careful might just find themselves as hooked on the sport as he. This may help to explain why sporting clays, often (sometimes ad nauseam) described as "golf with a shotgun," has been since its introduction into this country in the early 1980s probably the fastest-growing shooting sport. The National Sporting Clays Association (NSCA) has around 16,000 members and estimates that 300,000 shoot sporting clays regularly and 3 million shoot at least once a year on well over 1,000 different courses.

Sporting clays had its beginnings, innocently enough, in wing-shooting. In the beginning, apparently in the early 1920s, with live-pigeon shooting banned, British bird hunters began firing their bespoke guns at clay targets thrown to simulate the various flight patterns of the wild game they encountered in the field. At first, they did this to keep the rust off, if not improve, their hunting skills and to carry over the pleasures of the hunt into the closed season. As with so many harmless pastimes, though, this shooting was soon codified into a genuine sport with rules, competitions, and the inevitable winners and losers.

Shooting sporting clays.

Sporting clays. Clockwise (upper left): middi, standard, battue, rabbit. Center: mini.

In 1925, according to Britain's Clay Pigeon Shooting Association, one C. W. Mackworth-Praed won the first British Open Sporting, posting a score of 63 out of 80, venue unrecorded. By 1932, the Open was being held at the West London Shooting Ground, remaining a fixture there for generations. In 1963, the Open had its first American champion, S. Gulyas, breaking 84 out of 100.

By the sixties and seventies, based on the research of Georgia attorney Hugh Sosebee, Jr., and Dr. Robert Maurer, assorted flavors of "hunter's" clays were being shot from the East Coast to Sequim, Washington. It was sometime in 1983 or 1984 in the Houston area that the first rounds were shot of what actually called itself sporting clays and adhered to British rules—such as 100 targets per shooter per round, the targets being standard, rocket (similar in diameter, but thinner and faster), rabbit (same diameter, but rolls on the ground), battue (standard diameter, very thin, does wingovers), middi (3½-inch), and mini (2⅜-inch, resembles a hummingbird in a hurry) and shot from fixed stations in singles, and following, report, and true pairs with size 7½ shot or smaller. Today, sporting clays is shot on literally thousands of courses across the country and around the world.

As a measure of how challenging sporting clays can be, out of millions and millions of rounds shot, there have been only a handful of recognized perfect 100×100 rounds. In the National Sporting Clays Championship tournament, for example, a score of 190 out of 200 can often win the top prize, whereas in trap or skeet such a score wouldn't even get a shooter into the finals.

In order for you at least to feign comprehension of sporting clays the first time you step onto a course, you should know that the average recreational round generally consists of 100 birds for each shooter, shot at 10 different stations. There are, of course, variations of anywhere from 5 to 15 stations, or as few as 50 targets per round. Some courses have minimums, such as 200 birds per round, which may be shot by a single individual or divvied up among several shooters.

Shooters move through the course in squads, usually of five or six maximum. If you come alone or with just a friend or two, you may be grouped with other shooters to form a squad. Depending on the size of the squad and the course, a round can take from 45 minutes to 2 hours to complete. The score is recorded by the shooters on a score sheet with a hit marked with that universal "X" and a miss with the dreaded "O."

The stations are often named things like "Flighting Doves," "Flushing Quail," "Fur & Feathers," and so on, to indicate the type of winged game they are supposed to represent, although increasingly a target is thrown simply because, in one experienced shooter's words, it is a "neat target," and not for its theriomorphic qualities. Stations are, therefore, more likely to be just "Station 1" these days, rather than "High Driven Pheasant."

Once standing in a station, the shooter demonstrates both firearm safety and proper etiquette by not loading the gun until in position to shoot and ready to call for a target. The shooter should also never walk up to the station, or turn or walk away from it, unless the action of the gun is open and visible as such to the other shooters. The action should remain open between stations, and a shooter must be certain that the gun's muzzle is pointed in a safe direction at all times.

Etiquette also suggests that a shooter always have enough shells for each station, and have them handy, when stepping up to the station to prevent delaying the round by fumbling around while reloading. If the squad ahead is shooting slowly, don't crowd or disturb them with loud conversation. By the same token, if your squad is holding up another, let them "shoot through."

If someone's having a bad round, don't pour it on while he's shooting (that's what beers in the clubhouse are for). Likewise, if someone's smoking the course, don't jinx him by saying something stupid, like, "Gee, you can't miss!" because that's exactly what he'll do on the next shot. Also, refrain from offering free shooting advice unless asked.

Beyond basic gun safety and common courtesy, sporting clays remains a blessedly unregimented game. Of late, the only major rules question has been whether shooters have to adopt a low position with their gun, or if they can shoulder it before calling for a target. Presently, either position is acceptable.

Finally, there is the matter of cost. Not counting shells, a round of 100 birds at one of the tonier sporting-clays clubs in New York costs $100, after you've paid a $10,000 to $15,000 membership fee, in the hinterlands a 50-bird round might cost no more than $15.

If you can handle the financial end, then the single biggest obstacle to beginning sporting clays is bringing yourself to step onto a course the first time. Many novices, particularly women and younger people, are intimidated by the thought of a bunch of shotgun-wielding men snarling at them for *invading* the game. In fact, men these days are more than pleased to see new shooters; so in the words of the T-shirt: No fear!

If you've never shot clay birds (and frankly, even if you have), your first time on the sporting-clays course (or the trap or skeet field, for that matter) will be most profitably spent with an instructor. Gil Ash, who was mentioned earlier in connection with chokes, is a Level III instructor who conducts classes with his wife, Vicki, around the country. He recommends that beginners start out in an all-day group session, to provide a more intensive experience and to allow them to benefit from the instruction given other students, as well as from that which they receive.

Don't worry about a shotgun. (If you take away no other insight from this book, remember that the shotgun, or rifle or handgun, is secondary to beginning any of the shooting sports: Don't get hung up on the idea that you have to own the "right" firearm before you begin to shoot. Don't be afraid to begin with whatever you have, as long as it reasonably meets the requirements of the sport; and as you gain experience, you will come to know what you need.) A good instructor should have several shotguns to choose from, letting you find which suits you best. If you have your own gun, even if not an "official" sporting-clays model, bring it—as long as you are comfortable and can shoot doubles with it and it's open-choked, preferably Cylinder or Skeet. (Daniel Schindler, another Level III instructor, believes most clays shooters, like most trap and skeet shooters, overchoke, the "meat and potatoes" of sporting clays being 40-yard, or less, shots.)

Don't worry about your score, either, or even very much about breaking birds. A broken target is the result of the application of a series of fundamental shooting techniques and by itself is of far less import than grasping those fundamentals. Hits will outnumber misses soon enough.

Although we've discussed them previously, it is worth going over the fundamentals of shooting one more time, particularly as they apply to sporting clays. The first, of course is stance. Ideally, your body ought to be pointing, in the shooting position, toward the spot where the target can most easily be broken when the target reaches it. Because targets may travel in two directions at the same station in sporting clays (as doubles do in skeet), though, your stance should be relaxed and well balanced, but flexible.

In mounting the shotgun, the most fundamental thing you have to learn to do with your gun is raise, mount, and swing it in tempo with the target, *without* looking at the gun itself. It is "physically impossible," to quote Gil Ash, to look at the gun and the target and to expect to break the latter in any way but by accident. The key to hitting, again according to Ash, is "focusing on the front of the target" while bringing the comb of the gun firmly to your face.

Doug Fuller, 1997 National FITASC (*Fédération Internationale de Tir Aux Armes Sportives de Chasse,* the swifter, more rigid French version of sporting clays) champion, believes most misses can be diagnosed by the shooter's having lifted his head off the stock. Other faults include swinging the gun with your body rather than with your forward hand, or simply stopping the gun during its swing.

Properly mounting a shotgun can be practiced at home—**once again, always with an unloaded gun**—by bringing the gun up and tracing the line between the ceiling and the wall with the muzzle, your eye on the line, or by keeping your eye on a light switch or the corner of a picture frame as you mount the gun and point it at the spot. Hold the position for 10 seconds; if you look at the gun in that time, start again. Merely raising and mounting a shotgun for several minutes each day will build shooting muscles.

The best practice is, naturally, on a course. Sporting clays is first and foremost about fun, and the true fun lies in shooting a shotgun and knowing you can hit a target—seeing a bird break. If you shoot enough and break enough birds and you know why, then even the misses can be fun—because you realize they are nothing more than a learning experience, just another part of the game.

If you find yourself in a shooting slump or would like to post higher scores, the first thing to check is the basics: Are you still focusing on the front of the target? keeping your face on the stock? moving the gun with your hands and not your body? not stopping your swing? If none of these, let your instructor evaluate your shooting to see if the problem may be something you are unaware of. If all of your fundamentals are sound, then it may at last be time to look into a better gun to boost your percentage of hits.

The "perfect" gun is no substitute for proper technique in sporting clays or any other shooting sport. A shotgun with a good, for you, general fit, more open chokes, barrels not over 28 or 30 inches (too many shooters crave long barrels for those glamorous 50- and 60-yard crossing shots, which comprise a very small portion of sporting clays), and recoil you can tolerate through 100 shots are all you need in order to begin.

Later, when you want to move beyond that 70th or 75th percentile in your scoring, a handmade shotgun with an exact, custom fit, special triggers, trick chokes, and so on, *may* make a difference. Until then, there are a number of reasonably priced guns out there, one of which will certainly suit any sporting-clays shooter for years to come.

Any shotgun you choose won't be a hit without shells. Bargain-priced "field" loads may be no bargain; and "heavy" loads, over the course of 100 or 200 birds, are likely to damage the shooter more than the targets. Start with light target loads of 7½ to 8½ shot, then move up to more power as you see fit (this holds true for skeet and trap, as well).

Some shooters prefer paper-hulled shells because they perceive less recoil with them. Why? Theories include the shell's paper base-wads absorbing recoil, the paper crimp's opening easier, or the wad's sliding more smoothly against the waxed-paper wall of the hull—or all of the above, or none.

A day's worth of recoil is about the major health hazard connected with sporting clays, and the major health benefit is (as with all the shooting sports) mental, letting us (literally) blow away accumulated stress. Except for some "practical shooting" events we'll talk about in a later chapter, a round of golf—probably of *miniature* golf, at that—would provide a better workout. All it takes to participate in sporting clays is the stamina to shoot a shotgun, which means women (whom the Ashes estimate make up nearly a quarter of their new students), children, and even those in wheelchairs can enjoy it. Conditioning comes from repeatedly shooting that shotgun (though, as has been noted, mounting an empty gun, or curling 8- to 10-pound dumbbells, at home can also help build endurance).

The best way to think of sporting clays, in the words of one shooter, is that it "is a simple game shot by complicated people," which can be said of all the shooting sports. The less complicated we try to make ourselves, the more we can let clays reduce our stress—knocking targets out of the air does a far better job of this than chasing little white balls on the ground.

PART

II

Rifle and Pistol Sports

CHAPTER

7

To Be Precise

CCURACY is not an inherent quality of firearms. The earliest guns to fire single projectiles had smooth-bore barrels that enabled a shooter on a good day to hit a target roughly the size of a knight in armor mounted on a caparisoned horse as far away as 40 or 50 yards. (As inconsiderable a feat as that may sound, it came as such a shocking development to the ruling class in 17th-century Japan—who were horrified that a common foot soldier, a *peasant*, without the least spirit of *budo* or even any training in the martial arts, could kill a skilled samurai with one shot from a matchlock gun—that firearms were purposely abandoned in favor of the sword, the weapon of the nobility. This situation lasted until the early 1850s when Commodore Matthew Perry marched Japan into the modern era, literally at the point of a gun, or ship's cannon.)

Even though the smooth-bore shoulder gun had, according to the gunmaker W. Greener, a range that was "most contemptible"—a ball hitting the ground 120 yards after it left the muzzle—its ease of loading and the massed firepower it could provide made soldiers far more equal in battle than they had ever been with weapons requiring more expertise, and thus helped retain the musket as the standard small arm in warfare until nearly the mid-19th century. If nothing else, the gun made a good handle for a bayonet.

Accuracy in firearms came with the evolution of rifled barrels, beginning in the early 1500s, probably in Germany, and without any thought to their military application. Rifling in barrels was developed to help sporting marksmen hit targets.

The first riflings were designed as nothing more than gutters to collect excess fouling. Later, by calculation or random chance, it was determined that balls fired from barrels whose riflings were cut in a spiral pattern, or "twist," flew straighter. Archers had long known that they obtained greater accuracy with arrows and crossbow bolts whose fletchings, or whose vaned bolt heads, were angled to impart spin to the shafts in flight.This is simply the gyroscopic effect imparting greater stability to the projectile, letting it travel more smoothly through the air, a principle just as applicable to rifle balls.

Accurate rifles made target matches universally popular events in Europe, where one of the first known shooting clubs was started in the early 1600s in Geneva, and later in America. In the latter part of the 19th century, ranges began to be built on the East Coast just for target shooting. Facilities like What Cheer in Rhode Island and Creedmoor on Long Island even had target rifles and rounds, in calibers such as .40–90 and .44–100, named in their honor.

One type of target shooting, small bore, can be said to owe its existence to the military. The Army fitted the 1903 Springfield rifle with a .22 barrel to let troops practice marksmanship more economically and without the recoil of the .30-caliber round. Military-style shooting matches using standard-caliber rifles (the National Matches at Camp Perry, Ohio, being the most famous) are carried on extensively today, but the .22 probably predominates most shooting matches, and certainly Olympic style ones.

Shotgunning and biathlon aside, Olympic shooting involves three disciplines: rifle, pistol, and running target, the latter consisting of one event shot with air rifles. Air rifles and pistols also figure in the other disciplines, such as the air-rifle competition in rifle shooting. In the air-rifle event, a standing competitor uses a "free rifle" of .177 caliber to fire 60 shots in 1¾ hours at a .5-mm bull's-eye—the size of a period—at 10 meters. (All Olympic shooting events involve "free" rifles or pistols, that is, the firearms are not rested on a solid surface while being fired, but must be held by the shooter.) Except for running target, where scopes are used, only metallic sights are allowed. But rifles may have specially designed stocks, with hooked butt plates, palm rests, and weights on the barrel, whereas pistols may have baffles on the muzzles or grips that wrap completely around the hand, all to help improve shooting accuracy and, in the case of a top-of-the-line target rifle—which can weigh up to 17.6 pounds—set the shooter back about $3,000.

Olympic air pistol. *USA Shooting*

Olympic air rifle. *USA Shooting*

Olympic running target. *USA Shooting*

In running target, a shooter fires at a 10-meter target, with a 5-mm bull's-eye, the stupendous size of a pencil eraser, with a .177-caliber air rifle. The target moves across in front of him at two rates of speed, one that exposes the target to him for 5 seconds, the other at 2.5 seconds, and he fires 30 shots at each rate of speed.

The most fundamental rifle event, though, is the three-position using a .22 rifle. Here a competitor shoots at a dime-sized bull's-eye 50 meters away, firing 40 rounds from each of the three basic shooting positions: (1) standing, in which the shooter, leaning back with their feet slightly inside the shoulder width and the shoulders nearly perpendicular to the target, supports the rifle with the palm or extended fingers of the forward hand, held close to the trigger guard, while the elbow of that arm is pressed tightly into the body, all in order to reduce tremor; (2) kneeling, with the forward elbow hooked over the inside of the raised knee (no bone-to-bone contact of ulna on patella), the front foot turned in for better bracing; and (3) prone, with the elbows on the ground and the body lying at about a 45-degree angle to the target, legs in the most comfortable position for the shooter.

Comfort, or rather the avoidance of strain, is vital for accurate rifle shooting. Strain leads to fatigue and fatigue to tremors. Breath control is important, too. Take a deep breath, partially exhale, hold, then fire. *(Shooting Tip: Don't hold your breath—too long, that is; if you don't get the shot off within 5 or 6 seconds of partially exhaling, let all the air out, take another breath, and line up your sights again.)* Some shooters even try to time their shots between heartbeats so their bodies are completely still.

Knowing your rifle's exact trigger pull can let you do that. Shooters are always being told that it should be a surprise to them when the rifle goes off. And that makes a certain sense in terms of their not overanticipating the shot or flinching, but it does make it sound as though they're supposed to be just a big lump of dumb meat lying there. A skilled marksman, on the contrary, should know to the nanosecond when his rifle is going to fire, because it should not be even an instant before or after he intends it to. In *kyudo,* the Zen art of archery, it is said that an archer wants to develop the kind of muscle control that would let him use his "entire body to move just one finger." That's the sort of control a competitive target shooter wants to have, particularly in the pistol discipline that involves various rapid-fire and precision events, at ranges of from 25 to 50 meters, using .22s and air pistols, none of which, like the rifles, comes cheap.

Why do rifles and pistols and ammunition for target shooting cost so much?

Although proper technique significantly outweighs components (shotgun and shells) in successful shotgun shooting, target shooting demands far more of a balance between the two. Shotgunning, remember, involves trying to cover a flying disk with a 30-inch cloud of shot, whereas target shooting with a rifle or handgun can mean attempting to squeeze 5, 10, or even 30 bullets through the same hole. Timing, coordination, and a strong sense of spatial geometry all go into the shotgun sports; in target shooting it is stillness, precision, and concentration. For lack of a better word, shotgun shooting can be, and in some cases should be, looser than target shooting. The goal of target shooting is zero tolerance, in shooter and components alike.

This goal is exemplified in the manufacturing process used to produce target rifle and pistol ammunition. Rimfire .22 ammunition for target shooting, such as CCI's Pistol Match and its Green Tag, for rifle shooting, must undergo numerous "high-grading" steps before it goes on the market. Only the tightest-tolerance machines, involving the least amount of tooling, to avoid variations, can turn out potential match bullets, and then from those bullets only the best are chosen. The result may be that only one out of five bullets meets the standards of match grade, which in the case of the Green Tag ammunition means being able to produce groups with a maximum overall average of no more than .72 inches, based on five 10-shot groups shot at 50 meters, while with field or sporting ammunition, average groups of 1 to 2 inches are more usual. An added step CCI takes is to load its ammunition to subsonic velocities (although still within the range of the standard velocities required for target ammunition) in order to help reduce noise, recoil, and something perhaps not often thought of, the upset the bullet may undergo by passing through the sound barrier.

In ammunition for centerfire rifles, meant for hitting targets at 100, 200, 300, and even 1,000 yards, there is no alternative for exceeding the speed of sound, so tolerances must be even greater, over a wider range of components. The chain of events that goes into precision rifle ammunition begins with the purchase of the raw materials themselves, which must be of top quality. In the rifle bullet, the fundamental step is to have a jacket with as little variation as possible in the thickness of its wall. This means that after the steps involved in "cupping" the jacket (accomplished, essentially, by forming, through a series of deep draws, the jacket—made mostly of copper—into a con-

Pistol match and green tag ammunition. *Courtesy CCI*

tainer for holding the lead core), there will be no difference in the thickness of the wall at any latitude around it that is greater than .0003 inch. This is 3/10,000 of 1 inch, which in industrial terms is practically unmeasurable, versus about 8/10,000 variation in premium hunting bullets and up to 20/10,000 for average but entirely serviceable hunting bullets.

All of this is in service of making a bullet that approaches perfect concentricity, that will spin in flight exactly around its central axis without, in highly scientific terms, wobbling. But to get that bullet to fly right, every other component connected to it must have the same level of care applied to its manufacture and assembly. This includes cartridge cases with their own concentricity so they will fit exactly straight into the rifle chamber and so the powder will burn uniformly inside them. This means precisely the same measure of powder (with precisely the same rate of burn) poured into each case, along with match-grade primers that will ensure uniform ignition from shot to shot. Even the loading dies used for putting bullet, case, powder, and primer together must have their own strict tolerances or there is the risk of a finished cartridge being just that much off to make a bullet hit the target a fatal few tenths of an inch away from the point of impact of the other bullets. Each of these steps demands constant inspection and diligent quality control, and this requires more labor and consequently greater expense, which is why match-grade firearms and ammunition will cost generally twice as much as firearms and ammunition that are more than adequate for hunting needs.

In a sport like benchrest shooting, attention to detail must be lavished on every part of the rifle, from how true the barrel is bored down the dead center of the barrel blank to how strict the tolerances are in the riflings to how well the crown of the muzzle is finished off to how tightly the chamber holds the cartridge and how accurately it is aligned with the bore. There are also matters of how fast and how consistent is the lock time and how "clean" is the pull of the trigger— even on one set at the ethereal benchrest weight of 2 ounces. Is the scope reliable and properly mounted? Is there even the slightest irregularity in the stock, and is the bedding, as it was for Goldilocks, just right? And how well has the shooter maintained the rifle?

Such meticulousness (perfectionism, priggishness?) can undoubtedly make benchrest shooting look, to some, like the most robotic of the shooting sports; and there is no question that at the heart of the sport lies a certain single-minded obsession with repeating one act, that of firing a rifle, in exactly the same way, time and time again, all in the name of punching sharp, clean holes in a paper target. Yet we should never forget that one man's monotony is another man's Zen, and the object of benchrest shooting isn't to punch holes in a target at all: It is to punch one hole that, in the words of shooters, only gets "a little blacker" with each shot. (At the cosmic, postmodern end of precision shooting, carried out so far mostly in ballistics labs, paper targets have ceased to exist; shooters instead fire at some disembodied aiming spot down range, and the point of impact is determined acoustically by using four microphones to triangulate—*quad*rangulate?—its position, making it possible to measure groups that could not be gauged physically.)

No other shooting sport requires a working knowledge of more disciplines than benchrest shooting. In the service of trying to achieve that absolute mystic void of five bullets–one hole, that as yet unattained perfect group of .000 inches (although groups down to .05

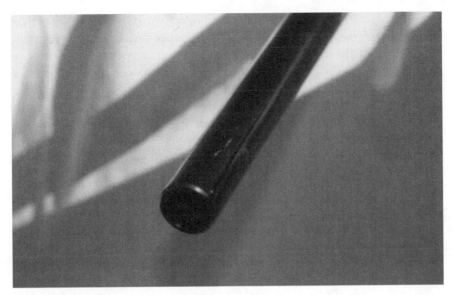

The crown of the muzzle.

inches, which is like having all the shots hit a bull's-eye smaller than the head of a pin, have been measured physically on paper targets), a shooter has to have at least a passing knowledge of physics, chemistry, physiology, meteorology, metallurgy, optics, and during competitions a dollop of psychology—and when he's squeezing off that fifth shot at a group that is nothing but a "bug hole," a little theology as well. Once sufficient experimentation has enabled him to find just the right combination of barrel, action, trigger, stock, optics, bullet, cartridge case, powder, and primer to make such bug holes possible by reducing potential mechanical error to the lowest levels attainable, then only human error remains, and that is where technique begins.

Even proper technique requires a few more components, though. As the name implies, benchrest shooting needs a bench to shoot off, and ranges where benchrest competitions are held will usually have benches made from solid concrete so there is no unsteadiness. *(Shooting Tip: Such rests may have little stools or seats to squat on. If you are going to be involved in a serious match or you are going to be spending some time practicing or working up a load, though, do yourself and your backside a favor by bringing a sturdy, solid folding chair you are comfortable in. And don't forget a cushion to sit on—benchrest is perhaps the one shooting sport in which a durable bottom is as important as a dead eye.)*

On top of the bench, another pair of rests are needed to support the rifle when fired. Keep two things in mind: Never rest a rifle on a hard surface, and never rest the rifle on the barrel. A hard surface can send bad vibes through a rifle when it's fired, upsetting accuracy; and resting a rifle on its barrel prevents the barrel from vibrating freely, which it does when a bullet is fired through it, exactly the same way shot to shot. The idea is to dampen any vibrations in the stock while allowing the barrel to oscillate naturally, and the best dampening medium is sand.

Loose sand, of course, isn't going to work, but sand in leather bags is remarkably effective. The pair of rests on the bench should support the rifle—in the rear under the toe of the butt and in the front under the fore-end. The front leather bag also needs to sit on a three-legged cast-metal pedestal that is adjustable for height. The front rest is adjusted to line the sights up for elevation, and even more for wind-age, whereas the rear rest fine-tunes elevation by being slid forward or back under the butt, raising or lowering the crosshairs in the scope. The shooter adjusts this rear rest with the nontrigger hand, whichever that may be, and lays that hand flat on the bench when shooting.

A benchrest shooter shoots with both elbows on the bench to maintain steadiness. Some shooters use a free-recoil style where virtually the only body part touching the rifle is the trigger finger. *(Shooting Tip: For any type of shooting, the finger should be placed on the trigger, not on the joint or out at the tip but between the first joint and the swirl of the fingerprint. This position transmits the least possible movement from the finger to the trigger.)* Others like to hold on for dear life. Either is a matter of preference, as long as a shooter can make certain his hold is unchanged from shot to shot. Similarly, after a rifle sustains recoil, the shooter must make certain that the rifle is repositioned exactly as it was before firing. This is sometimes accomplished by marking the spot on the fore-end where the rifle rests on the sand bag with a piece of tape; some rests have adjustable indicators that show where to slide the endcap of the stock out to before taking another shot. Beyond that, benchrest shooters have only to contend with their respiration, heartbeats, the muzzle blasts from the other rifles around them, wind, and mirage, which can make a target look like a penny sitting on the bottom of a wishing well.

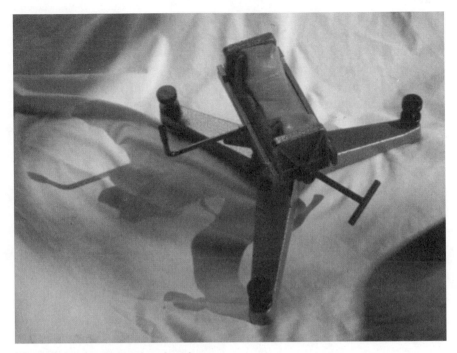

Three-legged cast metal pedestal rest.

Finger placement for proper trigger control.

One of the characteristics of benchrest rifles that make a free-recoil hold possible is that at their lightest they weigh 10½ pounds. According to the categories established by the two major benchrest organizations—the International Benchrest Shooters (IBS), which oversees benchrest shooting in the Northeast and overseas, and the National Bench Rest Shooters Association (NBRSA), begun over 50 years ago, which monitors the rest of the country—rifles may be Heavy Bench (or Unlimited), the only requirement being that they have at least an 18-inch barrel and a "safely operating firing mechanism"; otherwise they can be anything anybody can dream up; Heavy Varmint, same barrel length, but with a rifle stock and weighing no more than 13½ pounds; Light Varmint, the same as Heavy Varmint, but weighing no more than 10½ pounds; and Sporter, the same as Light Varmint, but not less than .23 caliber (there is also a "Hunter" category to provide an easy entry for newcomers into the sport by letting them compete with their deer rifles). Interestingly, the best five-shot groups, according to the IBS, have been shot not by the Unlimiteds but by Heavy and Light Varmints.

Where the Action Is

B ESIDES OLYMPIC and benchrest target shooting, there are numerous other free-rifle and free-pistol target sports, many using standard calibers, which are organized primarily by the National Rifle Association (NRA). There are even target matches for blackpowder rifles and pistols.

As the old Wild West shows knew, though, there is no great excitement in watching shooters, no matter the yardage or how intense the thrill is for the shooters, perforate paper. Almost all spectators, and not a few competitors, like nothing better than to hear a bullet hit something solid and, even better, to see something fall down. It was out of this motivation that metallic silhouette and practical shooting were born.

Both disciplines originated in the 1950s, one in Mexico and the other in California. The Mexican sport, *siluetas metalicas,* began with rancheros wagering on who could shoot a cull cow or sheep at the longest distance. By the time the sport moved north in the 1970s, silhouettes made from steelplate had, thankfully, replaced livestock, but the Spanish names for the former animate targets were retained. These include the *borrego,* or ram, the largest target, at approximately 27 inches tall and 32 inches long; the *guajalote,* or turkey; the *javelina,* or pig; and the smallest, at 11 inches by 10 inches, the *gallina,* or chicken, each with a welded-on base.

Metallic silhouette began as a rifle sport, and the targets were placed at appropriate, though longish, rifle distances: 500 meters for the sheep, 385 for the turkey (debates are endless over why 385 and not 400, because no one seems to know), 300 for the pig, and 200 for the chicken. All shooting is done off-hand, without any shooting aids such as slings or palm rests or even padded jackets or shooting gloves! Scopes are allowed, but no rifle may weigh more than 10 pounds, 2 ounces.

A shooter has 2½ minutes to fire at a bank of five of each target, and a complete match may consist of anywhere from 40 to 120 shots. To score a hit, a shooter must not merely strike the target but knock it completely off its stand.

It would seem that this ought to be a difficult enough task for any shooter, but as time went by the added challenge of trying to knock down targets with handguns steadily gained favor, coming eventually to eclipse the rifle version of the sport. In handgun metallic silhouette, the same targets are shot as with rifles, only at lesser distances: 200 meters for the sheep, 150 for the turkey, 100 for the pig, and 50 for the chicken. There are also rimfire and air-pistol versions of the sport at even shorter ranges and with smaller silhouette targets, as well as matches for rimfire and air rifles, and even events for old, blackpowder-cartridge buffalo guns, in which competitors may sit or kneel and use crossed-stick rests to shoot at bison silhouettes sometimes 700 or more yards away.

Left to right: *borrego, guajalote, javelina, gulliná.*

Production revolver.

Remington Model XP100R. *Remington*

Different classes of shooting are open, including Production Revolver in which a shooter may use only a stock handgun. Iron sights are generally used; but in the high-power, Hunter class guns, based mostly on the Remington XP-100 action and often extensively customized, scopes are allowed. More and more shooters in this class, though, are returning to iron sights, perhaps because they find them less nerve-racking than "chasing the wire around." *(Shooting Tip: Iron sights are aimed by visually centering the blade on the muzzle of the handgun in the "notch" of the sight at the rear of the gun, the top of the blade in line with the top of the rear sight. The target can either sit on top of the sight—known as a 6 o'clock hold—or be bisected by it—a dead-center hold—as long as the sights are properly adjusted for that type of hold and the shooter uses the same hold each time. Unlike with the shotgun, in pistol or rifle shooting the shooter focuses on the sights, letting the target blur.)*

In 1977, the International Handgun Metallic Silhouette Association (IHMSA) was founded. Today, it has some 6,000 members in locales as far-flung as Brazil and New Zealand. The widespread popularity of the sport may lie in there being no gray in it, no polite applause for a well-shot group, or any quiet sense of satisfaction. A shooter concentrates as hard as possible to hold his sights on the target for just an instant, touches off the shot, and then, after a noticeable pause, hears the unmistakable and thoroughly satisfying clang of a bullet solidly hitting steel. He then brings himself to look up and see that a target is gone and either hoots like a madman or maintains a smug and thoroughly artificial coolness.

Practical shooting is derived from military and law-enforcement training in the use of the handgun. In the 1950s, the likes of Jeff Cooper—one of the world's foremost handgunners, who today has more than 60 years of shooting experience—and other California shooters who had shot the military and law-enforcement courses, organized their own less formal "Leatherslap" competitions. The highlight of these was a head-to-head contest in which two shooters would draw and fire at balloons set at the normal combat-target range of seven yards. The first one to break a balloon won.

Out of these competitions evolved practical shooting, organized under the International Practical Shooting Confederation (IPSC) in 1976. In 1983, the U.S. branch of the IPSC, the U.S. Practical Shooting Association, was founded and now has 14,000 members nationwide.

The three elements of practical shooting, as stated in the IPSC's Latin motto, "*diligentia, vis, celeritas,*" are accuracy, power, and speed. Targets are 75 by 45 centimeters with 15-centimeter bull's-eyes. Targets are placed at combat distances, with a few as far away as 45 meters, and they must be shot at with full-power handguns (no smaller than 9 mm). Shooting is against the clock and often on the run, sometimes over and around obstacles. The only restrictions on targets are that the "course of fire be realistic and practical," although some shooting "stages" stretch credulity.

One classic practical-shooting stage is "El Presidente," which begins with the shooter facing away from three targets set 10 yards down range. At the signal, the shooter turns, draws, and fires twice into each target, reloads, and repeats the firing sequence—all in roughly 3 seconds. Handguns can be humble service revolvers, but in the unlimited competitions, where more and more speed is required to win and shooters bear a stronger resemblance every year to track and field athletes, the norm is now elaborately customized, scoped, $3,000 semiautos (known as race guns) straight from the *Men in Black* armory. These are handguns with little or no real-world application except to win contests. Practical shooters explain this by stating that their sport has "matured" beyond its "martial" origin, so that its only objective now is racking up the highest score, begging the question of why, then, the sport still insists upon calling itself practical.

CHAPTER 9

The Cowboy Way

THE FIRST REALLY ACCURATE HANDGUNS were dueling pistols, for good reason. Riflings were considered an "unfair" feature in the dueling pistol, though it is unlikely that they would have provided much advantage at the 12 to 16 paces at which most duels were fought. Even without riflings, because of the precision craftsmanship that went into their locks, sights, triggers, and stocks, dueling pistols were supremely accurate compared to the common handguns of the day and even to the first revolvers.

Practice with the dueling pistol was the first (most) serious type of target shooting with the handgun. The potential duelist would set up a cast-iron target, 3 feet in diameter, darkened with lamp black. To this target he would affix some two dozen "white wafers" (think of 18th-century Ritz crackers), then step back 14 or 15 paces and begin to fire, breaking the wafers one by one.

The duelist was advised to charge his pistol with just enough powder to cause the lead balls to flatten out to the "size of a shilling" when they hit the target. A shooter, after "presenting the pistol," should not "hesitate more than two or three seconds in aiming; for unless a man fires quickly he can never fire well." The serious duelist also added a man-sized target with a pistol attached to it. This pistol had a blank charge and a chord attached to the trigger. The chord ran back to the belt of the shooter, and as the duelist fired at his target, he would lean slightly backward, discharging the blank pistol. In this way he got used to shooting, and hitting, his target while under fire himself.

In the mythology of the Old West, the formal, aristocratic duel was transformed into the showdown, in which both combatants met in the dusty street at high noon and the winner was he who could "clear leather" first. Although during the days of the Western frontier, from 1850 to 1890, approximately 20,000 died in shootouts, almost none of these affairs looked anything like the opening credits of *Gunsmoke*. They were far more often short, violent, point-blank incidents that could erupt at the sight of a palmed ace or the utterance of a discouraging word. Alcohol played no small part in them, and they also involved a good bit of bushwacking. Rather than victory going to the fastest on the draw, it was far likelier that the cool-headed, or cold-blooded, gunman who could stand up and take aim while bullets flew around him would be the one who survived.

Nonetheless, the image of the fast draw (however false) remained an indelible one, especially after being immortalized in more than four generations of movie Westerns. In 1954, in *California* (stop me if you've heard this before), Dee Woolem, a stuntman at Knott's Berry Farm in Buena Park, decided to find out how fast a fast draw could be by setting up a large timer whose sweep second hand would be stopped by Woolem's breaking a balloon with his shot. What Woolem found was that a draw could be mighty fast.

The competitive fast draw today involves using a single-action revolver loaded wth blanks (or wax bullets). At a signal, the gunfighter draws the pistol, clears the holster, brings it level at waist height, and fans the hammer while holding back the trigger (in what has been described as "deliberate abuse" of the gun). The target is a 4-inch balloon, 8 feet away (with wax bullets it is a steel target set at 15 feet). The burning grains of blackpowder leaving the muzzle strike the balloon, breaking it and releasing a microswitch behind it, stopping the timer.

In a record fast draw, it takes .15 (15/100) second for the body to react to the signal, that is, for the sound to travel from the ear to the brain and for the resulting draw response to travel from there through the nerves to the gun hand. The actual drawing and firing of the pistol then takes less than .10 (10/100) second, sometimes considerably less, for a total time faster than a quarter second. Spectators are usually jumping at the gunshot before they realize the gun has been drawn.

Fast-draw competitions are organized by the World Fast Draw Association (WFDA). But for another group of shooters, there is the desire to carry the cowboy way beyond being quick on the draw. In the late

1970s in California (what *is* it with that state?), a group of pistol shooters who were admirers of everything about the Old West thought it would be fun to compete against one another with the 19th-century-style six-guns they all owned. At first, these were informal matches, and then shooters began adding traditional Western clothing and then period rifles and shotguns. Before they knew it they had a full-fledged adult fantasy on their hands, which in the last few years has doubled in size annually. They called the sport cowboy action shooting and established the Single Action Shooting Society (SASS) to organize it.

If you call the headquarters of the SASS to inquire about cowboy action shooting, don't be surprised if the pleasant-sounding woman who answers the phone identifies herself as "Poker Alice," the name of the not-so-pleasant cigar-chewing, campaign-hat-wearing, .45-wielding, stud-playing, English-born Deadwood madame. (Once asked how she had managed to pay back a bank loan well ahead of schedule, Alice is said to have replied that she'd known the Masons and the Grand Army of the Republic would be coming to town for conventions, but she'd plumb forgot to add in the Methodists.)

For quite some time now, of course, the bona fide Poker Alice has been, like Buffalo Bill, defunct. But a primary goal of the SASS is to preserve the spirit of the historical and mythological Wild West (including cinematic and television versions). One way they attempt to do so is by requiring members to assume the alias of a Western character with whom they feel they can identify. So it is no wonder that when the *faux* Poker Alice transfers your call, you're likely to find yourself speaking with one of the founders of the SASS, and proud wearer of badge #1, *"Judge Roy Bean"* (whose real name is . . . on second thought, let's just leave it at "Judge").

Besides aliases, cowboy action shooting requires clothing, firearms, and ammunition true to the Old West. Shooters compete with pistols, rifles (pistol calibers only, no .30–30s or '06s, and no velocities above 1,400 feet per second), and scatterguns in matches whose various stages strive to recreate scenarios of real and fictional Western shootouts. One typical scenario is a reenactment of the famous Indian attack scene in *Stagecoach* where the Duke (one of the credos of cowboy action shooting is that John Wayne could do no wrong) held off the Apaches with his trusty lever action from the roof of the stagecoach. (Another scenario that was tried early on, the dastard Jack McCall's foul gunning down of Wild Bill Hickok, was a flop:

Cowboy action shooting requires special "cowboy" loads. *Winchester*

Shooting anyone in the back, even a mannequin holding aces and eights, just was not the cowboy way, and the shootists were extremely reticent to participate.)

Shooters compete in classes for men and women ranging from junior to adult, in styles such as Modern (adjustable sights), Duelist (one-hand holds), and Frontiersman (blackpowder cap-and-ball pistols). Since the emphasis is, as the name implies, on "action" and not precision, targets are fairly large—about 16 inches by 16 inches—and are placed 20 to 30 feet away for pistols and 40 to 150 feet for rifles. Events are timed, with penalties added for misses. Awards are presented not only for shooting but also, as should come as no surprise, for best costumes.

The sport's main event is the World Championship of Cowboy Action Shooting "End of Trail," a four-day shootout held every year to determine the "Top Gun." Up to 600 competitors take part in the championship, which attracts over 15,000 spectators. Besides the regular stages, there are side matches for Derringers and fast draw and cowboy sporting clays. One of the most colorful and exciting side matches is the mounted shooting. In these a rider gallops through a course with 10 balloons set out along it. Using a .45 single-action

A cowboy action shooting stage or "scenario." *Photo by Ron Wolfson.*

Mounted shooting. *Photo by Ron Wolfson.*

loaded with specially prepared blanks, like those for shooting in fast draw, the rider tries to break each balloon while passing it, going for the best time with the fewest misses. In its way, it is a lot like the Wild West brand of *yabusame,* the Japanese sport of mounted archery. And so we seem to have come full circle in the shooting sports, and find ourselves going out the way we came in.

PART III

Parting Shots

10

The Beginning Battery

A S MENTIONED BEFORE, newcomers to the shooting sports seem to worry entirely too much about the kind of gun to use or buy and how much they should pay for it. Even greater than cost, though, is the concern they have about showing up with the "wrong" gun at the range and looking like a dork.

There is a temptation to try to calm such needless fears with vague generalities—essentially to soothe new shooters by saying, "There, there" instead of telling them what they really want to hear, the answer to the question, What should I buy? Merely saying that they ought to have a good 12-gauge shotgun, a reliable small-caliber target rifle, and an accurate small-caliber target pistol as their beginning battery for the shooting sports, without telling them *which* 12-gauge, rifle, or pistol, is like telling novice runners to get some shoes with rubber soles and, uh, nice laces.

The following, then, are specific and personal selections. Others may—in fact, will—offer differing opinions, some quite vehemently. This is only to be expected. Whichever firearm a new shooter eventually chooses, though, should be based on the criteria—at least in part—given here.

The firearm with the widest application for the beginner in the shooting sports is the shotgun. With the proper shotgun, a shooter may participate quite adequately in all the shotgun sports and have a gun to hunt with, if that is of interest to him. The new shooter, leery of recoil, may suppose that one of the subgauges, 20 gauge or less, is where to start. Subgauge shotguns are not for beginners, though,

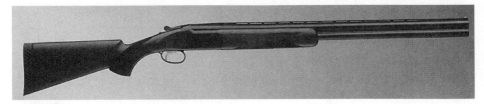

Browning Citori Sporting Hunter. *Browning*

Ruger Model 10/22 RB. *Ruger*

because they are highly likely to substitute frustration for recoil. The novice wants the largest possible pattern with the greatest number of pellets in the air when learning to break clay birds. This translates into a 12 gauge with a choke that is as open as is suitable for the game being shot. To counteract recoil, a shooter can look into lighter loads, to begin with, and into shooting vests or shoulder pads designed to absorb recoil.

As was suggested earlier, a 12-gauge over-and-under with barrels no longer than 28 inches and with interchangeable chokes is probably the best all-around choice for the shooter just getting involved in the shotgun sports. An ideal choice is the Browning Citori Sporting Hunter. Depending on how carefully you shop, you ought to be able to acquire a good new over-and-under for between $1,200 and $1,500 (be cautious about spending more than $2,000 for an over-and-under, especially if it is your first shotgun purchase). Bought right, an over-and-under, kept in good condition, will maintain much of its value, so if at some point you decide to sell it, you're not likely to be badly hurt.

For a first target rifle, the basic investment might be $200. This is because that rifle should be a .22, and the choice here is a Ruger 10/22. This semi-auto carbine is, out of the box, fine for plinking and

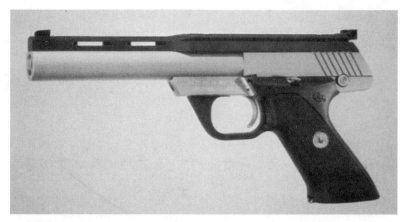

Colt .22 Target Model CC 5260. *Colt*

casual target shooting, as well as small-game hunting. One of the things about the 10/22, though, is that, being one of the most popular small-arms rifles on the market, it has had a vast array of after-market accessories grow up around it, so that the factory rifle you buy can just be the starting point to building and customizing a precision target rifle. Target barrels, stocks, triggers, and so on, can all be easily adapted to the 10/22; one of the best sources for these products is Butler Creek [phone (503) 655-7964].

With distinctive lines, a comfortable, solid feel in the hand, target sights, and a reliable semi-auto action, the Colt Woodsman was one of the finest pistols ever built. Long discontinued, Colt nonetheless carries over many of the Woodsman's best features in its .22 Target CC5260 pistol. This is another sensible choice, not only for introductory target shooting and plinking but also as a handy sidearm for the trail or the hunt, for collecting small game for the dinner pot in camp. The CC5260, priced around $377, represents a not insubstantial investment; but .22 ammunition remains one of the genuine bargains in the world today, with less than $2 buying a beginner 50 rounds for practice. And not only are .22s inexpensive to shoot, they also eliminate any concern about recoil and allow a shooter to concentrate on perfecting form. Once that has been accomplished, the novice can begin to think about different calibers and more specialized firearms and having them customized.

11

The Future

I N ORDER FOR THE BEGINNER and the veteran alike to practice the shooting sports, they need to have access to firearms. It would be nice if it were possible to write about the shooting sports without having to discuss the potential impact firearms' laws may have on such access and on the ability to use sporting guns. However, the movement toward greater restrictions on the use of firearms will eventually have its effect, and those who participate in them now, or hope they will in the future, need to be prepared for what lies ahead if they wish to see the shooting sports continue.

While just 14 percent of the general public, according to a 1996 NSSF poll, believe there should be no private ownership of firearms for any purpose, the remainder of the population is hardly monolithic in its support of gun possession. Among this wide majority, opinion ranges from the "cold-dead-fingers" school of the absolute right to bear arms to a far squishier acceptance of the notion of permitting certain firearms to be used only in supervised and regulated competitions. Even someone who competes with a .45 semi-auto pistol and keeps the gun at home for self-defense often feels uneasy about trying to defend either the utility or the application of a shoddily made, extremely inaccurate, and easily concealed .25.

The justifiable ambiguity almost all of us feel about at least some firearms is what sanctions an inevitable trend of gun-control laws toward increasing restrictions on the private ownership of all firearms. And it is not simply restriction because the final, though unspoken, objective of the most ardent advocates of control is the eventual banning of all firearms, no matter what use they might be put to. The argument that firearms employed primarily in the shooting sports pose practically no threat of ever being used in a criminal manner always falls on deaf ears wherever more draconian gun laws are enacted. Recently, in such fiercely democratic countries as England and Australia, the banning trend has seen the outlawing of semi-auto shotguns (good-bye, 200-target rounds of sporting clays) and all handguns (farewell, practical shooting, cowboy action shooting, handgun metallic silhouette, even Olympic pistol shooting). Canada has gone so far as to regulate the ownership of certain types of crossbows.

In this country there is no question that what has stood in the way of the more flagrant excesses of gun control has been one organization. Love it or hate it—and there are ample reasons for doing both—the National Rifle Association has been the single force that has kept gun ownership as relatively free in this country as it is, and by so doing it has made it possible for the shooting sports to continue to flourish.

The NRA works to combat not only the direct loss of gun rights but numerous end-runs as well. Among these are laws and ordinances forbidding the discharge of firearms in areas in which such shooting has traditionally been allowed; liability laws that are nothing more than veiled means of penalizing arms and ammunition manufacturers for the intentional misuse of their products, the ultimate goal being death by lawsuits for the firearms industry; and even environmental laws that dubiously target shooting ranges as sources of pollution in order to shut them down and further limit access to the sporting use of firearms.

Vital and popular shooting sports—something the NRA also works to organize and encourage—represent a powerful force in support of the continued private ownership of firearms. If the shooting sports, with their millions of participants (and millions of votes), were to disappear tomorrow morning, by tomorrow afternoon the proponents of far more rigid gun control would be pressing their case with exponentially great force. The individual shooting sports cannot continue to exist on their own, though, oblivious to political reality and to the subtle, and often insidious, ways in which public opinion is shaped. To survive they must speak out in a single, clear voice.

The NRA provides such a voice because it is the one organization that concerns itself directly and vigorously with the issues that affect firearms and shooting. Can the NRA be exasperating, troglodydtic, dumb as a stump, or sometimes not a little ridiculous? All of the above. Yet, anyone who wants to carry on in the shooting sports, and has hopes of passing the tradition along, must strongly consider what alternative there may be to joining and supporting the NRA and its activities.

CHAPTER

Final

RATHER THAN ENDING this book on a solemn note, let it instead be ended on a serious one. It needs to be said again, and it cannot be said too often, what the shooting sports are all about—more than competition or scores or medals—is play.

What, is play to be taken seriously? To see what a truly serious business it can be, just look at the faces of children when they are absorbed in play and have been transported to somewhere far outside themselves or so deep within themselves that they have no

Shooting is about fun as much as competition. *USA Shooting*

words to describe it. If we look at the shooting sports as *games,* rather than, more pretentiously, as *disciplines;* if we can for a while go beyond our dreary adult natures that demand structure, order, and *purpose* in every aspect of our lives, and remember what it once was like to do something solely for the fun of it—in fact, not even to "have" fun but simply to throw ourselves into a game and let the fun well up around us on its own—if we can come to understand that the shooting sports are worth doing simply because they are *neat* things to do; then, yes, it is entirely possible to take play as seriously as a child, and to see that the shooting sports are among the most serious, and least solemn, forms of play we can enjoy. In the end, there is just no way to remain solemn about something that is always going *Bang!*

13

Resources

A GOOD INFORMATION SOURCE for all the shooting sports is *GunGames Magazine,* published bimonthly and covering the waterfront, or rather the range of shooting disciplines. A year's subscription is $16.95. *[Call (909) 485-7986 for subscription information.]*

If you're interested in learning about trap and skeet, most shotgun ranges rent guns and have instructors to teach you the fundamentals. For a comprehensive listing of trap, skeet, and sporting-clays ranges across the country, as well as information on more advanced wingshooting courses, pick up a copy of *Black's Wing & Clay [$14.95, plus $4 shipping and handling; (732) 224-8700]*, a guide to shotgun equipment, instruction, and destinations. Some of the larger shotgun-shooting courses, held at various locations around the country, are Browning Instinctive Target Interception Shooting School *[(505) 836-1206]*, Holland & Holland Sporting Weapons Limited *[(212) 752-7755]*, Orvis Shooting Schools *(1-800-548-9548)*, The Remington Shooting School *(1-800-742-7053)*, and Sporting Classics Wingshooting School Presented by Beretta *(1-888-636-8654)*, or check with any of the shotgun organizations listed here.

For introductions to the various rifle and pistol games, besides contacting the organizations listed, ask at your nearest gun shop or police or sheriff's department for the location of rifle and pistol ranges and clubs in your area, or check the NRA, the final authority on all matters gun.

The organizations mentioned in this book can be contacted directly:

ATA
601 West National Road
Vandalia, Ohio 45377
(937) 898-4638
Fax: (937) 898-5472
Website: www.shootata.com

FITASC
10, rue de Lisbonne
Paris, 75008
FRANCE
011-33-1-4293-4053
Fax: 011-33-1-4293-5822

IHMSA
P.O. Box 368
Burlington, Iowa 52601
(319) 752-9623
Fax: (319) 753-1312
Website: www.ihmsa.org

IPSC
P.O. Box 972
Oakville, Ontario
L6J 929
CANADA
(905) 842-6960
Fax: (905) 842-4323
Website: www.ipsc.org
E-mail: info@ipsc.org

NBRSA
2835 Guilford Lane
Oklahoma City, Oklahoma
    73120-4404
(405) 842-9585
Fax: (405) 842-9575

NRA
11250 Waples Mill Road
Fairfax, Virginia 22030
(703) 267-1000
Fax: (703) 267-3909

Membership: 1-800-NRA-3888
    or (703) 267-3730
Website: www.nra.org

NSSA and NSCA
5931 Roft Road
San Antonio, Texas 78253
(210) 688-3371
Fax: (210) 688-3014

NSSF
11 Mile Hill Road
Newtown, Connecticut 06470-2359
(203) 426-1320
Fax: (203) 426-1087
Website: www.nssf.org
E-mail: info@nssf.org

SASS
1938 North Batavia
Suite M
Orange, California 92865
(714) 998-1899
Website: www.sassnet.com
E-mail: sasseof@aol.com

SCA
9257 Buckeye Road
Sugar Grove, Ohio 43155-9632
(740) 746-8334
Fax: (740) 746-8605

UIT
Bavariaring 21, D-80336
Munich 1
GERMANY
011-49-89-5443550
Fax: 011-49-89-5435544

USA Shooting
One Olympic Plaza
Colorado Springs, Colorado 80909
(719) 578-4670
Fax: (719) 635-7989

USPSA
P.O. Box 811
Sedro Woolley, Washington 98284
(360) 855-2245
Fax: (360) 855-0380
Website: www.uspsa.org

WFDA
P.O. Box 247
Vernonia, Oregon 97064
(503) 429-4181
Fax: (503) 429-8032

E-mail:
    oregondrifter@vernonia.com

WSSF
4620 Edison Avenue
Suite C
Colorado Springs, Colorado
    80915
(719) 638-1299
Fax: (719) 638-1271
Website: www.wssf.org
E-mail: wssf@worldnet.att.net

Glossary

action—mechanism which the barrel screws into that supports the rear of the **cartridge;** the action loads the cartridge into the **chamber,** fires it through the **trigger** and **firing pin,** and unloads the empty **case.**

ATA—Amateur Trapshooting Association, the governing body for trapshooting in the United States.

auto-loading—or "automatic": See **semi-automatic.**

barrel—tube through which a projectile is fired from a firearm.

barrel blank—steel stock into which the **bore** is drilled.

battue—sporting-clays target that rises straight into the air, usually thrown in true **pairs;** named for the European form of driven hunting in which the game jumps up in front of the hunter.

bead—globular metal sight set on top of the **barrel** of a shotgun or rifle, usually near the **muzzle.**

bore—most simply, the cylindrical interior of the **barrel;** in rifles the term also designates the diameter between the tops of the **lands** of the **rifling,** by which the rifle's **caliber** is often defined; in shotguns, the **gauge.**

break action—a gun that opens and closes by means of a lever and a hinge mechanism.

Break action.

breech—rear end of the **barrel,** behind the **chamber.**

breech loader—firearm that loads from the **breech,** usually by use of a **cartridge;** see **muzzle loader**.

bullet—projectile fired from the **barrel** of a rifle or handgun.

butt—rear of a rifle or shotgun **stock;** the part held against the shoulder.

caliber—diameter of **bore,** designating **bullet** size, for example, .30 caliber, .30-inch-diameter bore.

cartridge—the assembled **case, primer, powder** (plus the **wad** in shotgun cartridges) and projectile that are loaded into a firearm and fired by the **action;** in shotguns, the cartridge is sometimes called a shotshell.

case—container, usually brass in rifles and handguns and paper or plastic in shotguns (where it is more often called a hull), which holds **primer, powder,** and the projectile that make up the **cartridge**.

cast—slight sideways bend or twist in the shotgun **stock** to bring the **rib** into more direct alignment with the shooter's eye when the gun is shouldered.

chamber—portion of a firearm, usually in the end of the **barrel** in the **action** (revolvers are an exception), which contains the **cartridge** for firing.

choke—minor constriction of the **muzzle** of a shotgun to increase the density of the shot **pattern,** thereby increasing the gun's effective range.

choke tubes—interchangeable tubes that screw in or out of the shotgun **muzzle** and provide varying degrees of **choke**.

clay target—or clay pigeon or clay bird. Generally, a domed disk made from petroleum pitch and gypsum that is thrown through the air to create a flying target for shotgunners; clay targets come in a standard size (108 mm in diameter), as well as in **middi, mini, rabbit,** and **battue**.

comb—top edge of the rear of a rifle or shotgun **stock;** the portion of the stock upon which the shooter's cheek rests.

crown—end of the rifle or handgun **barrel** surrounding the **muzzle;** a crown properly finished and free of any imperfections can greatly aid accuracy.

dominant eye—the eye that controls vision; that is, one eye, either right or left, is usually more "powerful" than the other and does more of the seeing, just as one hand is stronger than other and does more of the work.

double-barrel—firearm with two parallel **barrels** aligned either **side-by-side** (on a horizontal plain) or **over-and-under** (on a vertical plain); sometimes called a double or double gun.

doubles—see **pairs**.

drop—downward bend in the stock to bring the shotgun **rib** or rifle sight to eye level when a shooter shoulders the firearm.

dry fire—practice with an unloaded firearm.

earmuffs—hearing protectors which completely cover the ears.

firing pin—pin or plunger that strikes the **primer** in a **cartridge** when the firearm's **trigger** is pulled.

FITASC—**Fédération Internationale de Tir Aux Armes Sportives de Chasse,** the organizing body for the French version of sporting clays.

flintlock—muzzle-loading firearm whose source of ignition is a flint, held in the jaws of the gun's **hammer,** that strikes a **frizzen** and creates sparks that fall onto the priming **powder.**

following pair—see **pairs**.

fore-end—front portion of a firearm's **stock** gripped by the shooter's forward hand.

fowler—a **muzzle loader,** usually 12 gauge or larger, used for hunting waterfowl, or a person who hunts waterfowl.

free-floated—rifle barrel that does not come into direct contact with the **stock**.

free pistol—also free rifle. A style of pistol (or rifle) shooting in which no rests are used; also, a pistol (or rifle) relatively free of any design restrictions.

free-recoil—style of benchrest shooting in which the shooter makes little or no contact with the rifle other than with the **trigger** finger.

frizzen—steel blade, part of the **lock** of a **flintlock,** that is struck by flint, the flint scraping off splinters of white-hot steel, which fall into the pan holding the priming **powder,** igniting it.

gauge—inner diameter of a shotgun **barrel** based on the number of balls of pure lead of that size that will equal 1 pound; for example, twelve 12-gauge balls of lead equal 1 pound; the .410 is the one shotgun defined by **caliber** rather than gauge.

grip—narrow portion of the **stock** behind the **action** that is held by the **trigger** hand.

groove diameter—diameter between the bottoms of the **grooves** in **rifling;** this is also the actual diameter of a **bullet,** as opposed to its **caliber;** for example, a .30-caliber bullet is actually .308 inches in diameter, thus allowing the **lands** of the rifling to grip it when it is fired down the **barrel**.

grooves—spiraling channels cut into the rifle **bore;** see **rifling**.

hammer—essentially, an external striking device on any firearm that when released by the pulling of the **trigger** falls on the **frizzen,** or **percussion** cap, or the **firing pin,** instituting ignition.

heel—top end of **butt**.

IBS—International Benchrest Shooters, the governing body for benchrest shooting on the East Coast and internationally; see **NBRSA**.

IHMSA—International Handgun Metallic Silhouette Association.

IPSC—International Practical Shooting Confederation, the international organization for practical shooting; see **USPSA**.

lands—spiraling ridges between **grooves** in the rifle **bore;** see **rifling**.

lead—the distance ahead of a moving target that a firearm must be pointed in order for its projectile or projectiles, when fired, to intercept the target.

length of pull—measurement of the length of the rear of the **stock** that can be taken at three points: from the **trigger** to the **heel;** from the trigger to the center of the **butt;** from the trigger to the **toe**. The length of pull varies for each shooter, depending on physique.

lock—firing mechanism of a firearm, including **trigger, hammer** or **striker,** and **firing pin;** or the external firing system, such as on a **flintlock**.

lock time—interval between pulling the **trigger** and having the **firing pin** strike the **primer;** the faster the better.

magazine—the part of a firearm that holds extra **cartridges,** from which they can be loaded into the **chamber**.

middi—clay target smaller (90 mm in diameter) than standard, used in sporting clays.

mini—smallest (60 mm in diameter) clay target, used in sporting clays.

Monte Carlo stock—stock with **comb** raised above **heel** to allow the shooter to hold the head higher and straighter on the gun.

musket—smoothbore shoulder firearm, the principal infantry small-arms weapon until the mid-1800s, named for the male sparrow hawk.

muzzle—the forward end of the firearm **barrel** from which a projectile is fired.

muzzle loader—firearm in which **powder** and a projectile are loaded through the **muzzle** and tamped down into the **chamber;** see **breech loader**.

NBRSA—National Bench Rest Shooters Association, Incorporated, the national benchrest shooting organization for areas outside the East Coast; see **IBS**.

NRA—National Rifle Association.

NSCA—National Sporting Clays Association, the larger of the two national sporting clays organizations; see **SCA**.

NSSA—National Skeet Shooting Association.

NSSF—National Shooting Sports Foundation, a shooting-industry trade organization.

off hand—shooting from the standing position without the use of a rest or aid.

Off hand. *Remington*

over-and-under—see **double-barrel**.

pairs—two **clay targets** thrown together; "true"—targets thrown simultaneously; "report"—second target thrown at sound of shot at first target; "following"—second target thrown immediately after first.

pattern—expanding area covered by a load of shot after it leaves the **muzzle** of a shotgun; also called spread.

percussion—form of firearm ignition using an explosive **primer** that can be detonated by being struck, as with a **hammer**.

plinking—informal, casual shooting at targets such as empty cans, plastic jugs, old fruit and vegetables.

ports—a series of vents machined into the **muzzle** of a firearm that direct the exhaust gases that pass through them out the sides of the muzzle, helping to lengthen the period of **recoil,** and therefore lessen its sensation; also called a muzzle brake.

powder—explosive or inflammable propellant that when ignited produces expanding gases that drive a projectile from the **barrel** of a firearm.

primer—explosive cap or **powder** used to ignite the main powder charge in firearm.

pump—type of action that loads and unloads the **cartridge** by means of a manually operated slide.

recoil—rearward force exerted by a firearm when fired.

rib—metal band along the top of the **barrel** used as a sighting plain.

rifling—spiral **grooves** and **lands** in the **bore** that impart spin, and stability, to a projectile when fired.

safety—lock on the **action,** activated by a switch or button, which when in use prevents the **trigger** from being pulled or the **striker** from falling when the firearm is cocked.

SAAMI—Sporting Arms and Ammunition Manufacturers' Institute; sets standards for firearms and ammunition.

SASS—Single Action Shooting Society, the governing body for cowboy action shooting.

SCA—Sporting Clays of America, the smaller of the two national sporting clays organizations; see **NSCA**.

shot size—differing diameters of lead shot used in shotguns; sizes range from No. 9 at approximately .08-inch diameter to No. 2 at .15-inch to buckshot, the diameter of pistol bullets.

Shot Size	Shot Diameter		2 oz.	$1\frac{7}{8}$ oz.	$1\frac{5}{8}$ oz.	$1\frac{1}{2}$ oz.	$1\frac{3}{8}$ oz.	$1\frac{1}{4}$ oz.	$1\frac{1}{8}$ oz.	1 oz.	$\frac{7}{8}$ oz.	$\frac{3}{4}$ oz.	$\frac{1}{2}$ oz.
#9	●	.08	1170	1097	951	877	804	731	658	585	512	439	292
#8	●	.09	820	769	667	615	564	513	462	410	359	308	205
#7½	●	.095	700	656	568	525	481	437	393	350	306	262	175
#6	●	.11	450	422	393	337	309	281	253	225	197	169	112
#5	●	.12	340	319	277	255	234	213	192	170	149	128	85
#4	●	.13	270	253	221	202	185	169	152	135	118	101	67
#2	●	.15	180	169	158	135	124	113	102	90	79	68	45

Approximate number of shots in various loads. Courtesy of *Black's Wing & Clay*.

side-by-side—see **double-barrel**.

smoothbore—firearm without **rifling** in the barrel.

stage—target presentation or shooting scenario in cowboy action or practical shooting competitions.

stand—also called station. Individual shooting position or target presentation in the shotgun disciplines or games.

stock—"handle" that holds the firearm **action** and **barrel;** in a pistol, the stock may be only the **grip,** whereas in a rifle or shotgun the stock includes the **fore-end, grip, comb,** and **butt;** a stock may be wood, synthetic, or even metal.

striker—internalized part of the **action** which hits the **firing pin** when the trigger is pulled.

toe—bottom point of the **butt**.

trap—originally, the box used to hold a live pigeon, which was then released as a target in a shooting match; today, any machine used for throwing a **clay target;** also, an abbreviated term for trapshooting.

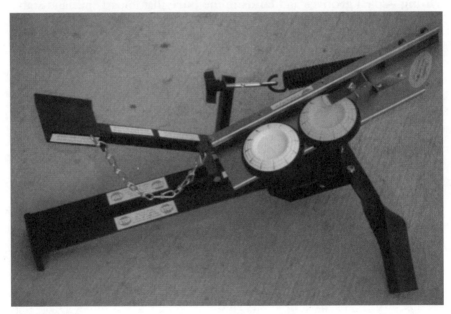

A Trius trap.

traphouse—structure in which the **trap** is contained, out of sight of shooters; a structure serving a similar purpose in skeet is known as a skeethouse.

trapper—individual who releases **trap,** either manually or electronically, when a shooter calls for a target.

trigger—lever for releasing the sear that holds the **hammer** or **striker** in the cocked position.

trigger guard—loop that encircles the **trigger** and helps to prevent accidental discharge.

UIT—Intrernational Shooting Union.

USA Shooting—U.S. Olympic shooting organization.

USPSA—U.S. Practical Shooting Association; see **IPSC**.

wad—spacer, made of fiber or plastic, placed between the **powder** and the shot to create a seal over the powder and to act as a piston when the powder is ignited, pushing the shot out of the **barrel**.

HULL
The outer container of a shotgun shell, typically made of plastic with a metal base.

SHOT
Round projectiles, usually of lead or steel. Depending on shot size and load, a shell can contain from 45 to 1,170 shot.

WAD
Plastic or fiber separating powder and shot that forms a seal so that gasses eject shot uniformly down the barrel.

POWDER
Gun powder situated above the primer where it will be ignited by the flames caused by the detonation of the primer compound.

PRIMER
A compound contained in the middle of the base of a shotgun shell, where the firing pin strikes.

Wad. Courtesy of *Black's Wing & Clay.*

WFDA—World Fast Draw Association.

WSSF—Women's Shooting Sports Foundation.

Index

EAU CLAIRE DISTRICT LIBRARY